City Science

City Science

Peggy K. Perdue
Diane A. Vaszily

Illustrated by Karen Waiksnis DiSorbo

GoodYearBooks
An Imprint of ScottForesman
A Division of HarperCollins*Publishers*

To Chris Jennison — without his gentle push, this book wouldn't have been written.
— P.K.P.

To the memories of my years at Madison Elementary School in York, Pennsylvania.
— D.A.V.

Good Year Books are available for preschool through grade 6 and for every basic curriculum subject plus many enrichment areas. For more Good Year Books, contact your local bookseller or educational dealer. For a complete catalog with information about other Good Year Books, please write:

Good Year Books
Scott, Foresman and Company
1900 East Lake Avenue
Glenview, Illinois 60025

Printed in the United States of America.

ISBN 0-673-46430-X

1 2 3 4 5 6 7 8 9 10-VPI-99 98 97 96 95 94 93 92 91 90

An Imprint of ScottForesman
A Division of HarperCollins*Publishers*

Preface

Children often think that nature is the park, forest, or zoo, and to experience nature they must travel to these places. They don't realize that nature is right outside, whether it be a school playground, a backyard, or a city street. Because science is everywhere also, nature and science cannot help but go hand in hand. To those who think that science is not something they can study in the city or that science belongs in a science lab, we present a new perspective, *City Science.*

Even though some of the activities in this book are well known, the Focus and the Extension activities place them in a new light. Throughout *City Science,* the student is provided with opportunities not only to explore scientific or ecological principles, but to understand how these apply to the interdependency of all life.

The style presented in *City Science* is easy to follow. Once familiar with the purpose behind this book and the design of the explorations, the teacher will be able to take ideas, both old and new, and put them into the same framework. Students will experience the relevancy of science. Science is no longer another activity designed to fill the allotted time, but a tool to bring into focus why life exists as we know it.

Does your science curriculum need a breath of fresh air? It is time to see science where it exists... naturally. Go outside to explore water droplets, investigate under trees, observe silhouettes, and study the sounds trapped within the city. Go outside today! It's time for *City Science.*

Table of Contents

Earth Science Activities

Environmental Science Activities

Life Science Activities

Physical Science Activities

Survey Science Activities

Appendix

How to Use This Book

If you have felt confined inside for science, *City Science* is just what you need to turn your schoolyard into your science classroom. Investigations include earth, environmental, life, physical, and survey sciences. The labs are independent of each other and can be used in any order, based on your needs and preferences.

City Science should be used by field teams of three or four students, unless the activities are being used at a learning center for individual use. The activities found in this book are designed for students in grades Three through Five, although they have been used with all ages of elementary students in all types of schools.

Each activity is prefaced with a brief, concise rationale to help you focus on the main intent. It will assist you in deciding the order of the activities. Relevance to Everyday Life provides the key to the entire "web of science" and offers you the avenue for integrating the specific activity into a much larger scheme. Be sure to include this aspect in your discussions with the class. It is important for students to see science as "everything that surrounds them" and not just a time frame in the daily curriculum schedule. To be truly relevant, science must have a personal impact on students.

The supplies needed for the activity are listed under Materials. You will need to provide enough for each field team. If investigations are presented individually, the materials could be at a learning center ready for the student to use. If multiple investigations are offered, or if space is limited, the materials could be labeled and stored and the student made responsible for gathering and returning them.

Suggested procedures for each investigation are presented under "How to Do It." Any advance preparation that may be needed is outlined under this heading. Your students may be capable of the preparation themselves. This is a goal you will want to strive to attain as the year advances. While students in grades Kindergarten through Sixth have successfully completed these activities, slight modifications may be necessary for your specific class.

We consider Data Collecting and Recording to be a vital aspect of any lab experience. Students should be encouraged to make and keep Observation Books. Guidelines are given in the section entitled Developing Observation Books.

The Extension Activities can be used to integrate other subject areas with the investigation, thus extending that "web of science." More importantly, these activities will help encourage creative problem solving and can be expanded into a unit of study. Extension activities may be assigned, or students may choose one. Additional extensions designed by the student teams could be kept on file for future use.

Developing Observation Books

Observations take on new meaning once they are recorded. Such a record not only allows students to remember the activities and refer to them at a later date, but invites comparisons with other scientists carrying out the same type of work. Data Collecting and Recording allows the recording of observations in a variety of ways.

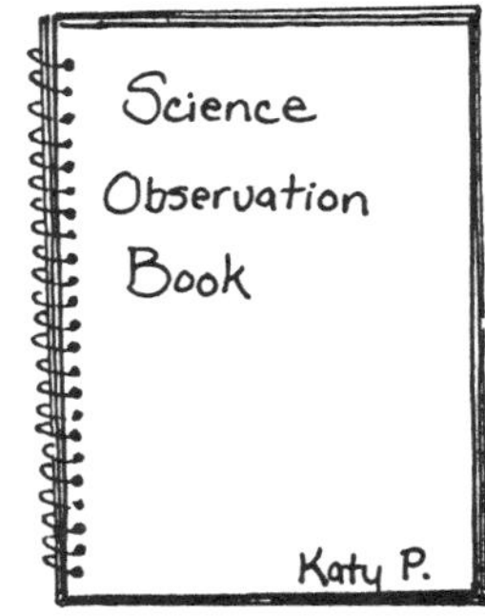

Drawings, charts, graphs, and photographs are the most common ways to record data. While students may need assistance initially in setting up charts and graphs, it is important that they begin designing their own as soon as possible. Constructing charts and graphs is an excellent way to integrate science and mathematics. The construction process also leads to a greater understanding when graphs and charts are studied in social studies.

This strategy most closely resembles the way research scientists and naturalists actually work. It encourages creative thought on the part of each student, even though they are working within teams. Students should NEVER be without their Observation Books when they are "doing" science!

Designing the Observation Book

Although cooperative learning is the method of choice for carrying out the activities in this book, Observation Books should be individually kept. A team of three or four working together may delegate responsibilities and keep a team record, but each student should keep an individual record as well.

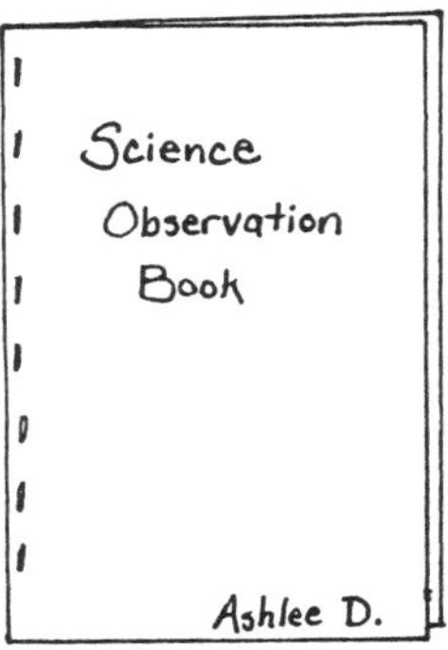

Observation Books should be bound together in a sturdy fashion and used ONLY as observation books for science. Discourage use of a multiple-notebook approach. Students could buy notebooks for this purpose (ideal size is 9" x 6") or make them from folded plain pieces of letter size paper (8 1/2" x 11"). Ten folded pages will give each student 40 pages of observations. A piece of construction paper, 60-pound paper, or samples from a wallpaper book can serve as front and back covers. Use staples, brads, or small rings for binding.

Using the Observation Book Pages Provided

Although we highly recommend constructing your own Observation Books, sometimes schedules just do not allow for such creativity. If you find yourself in this situation, observation pages for each activity have been included. This will standardize the Observation Books among the teams and produce more uniform results, but will reduce the opportunity for team creativity. After using these pages for the first few activities, or even for the first year, we know you will want to encourage some creative data collecting.

What to Include in the Observation Book

A Table of Contents in the front of the Observation Book will help students locate information quickly. Simply leave the first two pages blank and fill them in as you go. Be sure to number the pages in the book as they are completed!

The activity name and date should always be included on each page of the Observation Book. Each activity has a section entitled *Data Collecting and Recording*, which suggests the type of information that should be collected. You may find it helpful to discuss the method of recording data that would work best with each activity. Initially, you may even want to use a standard design. With subsequent activities, begin to allow individual planning and creative thought among the "scientists." At the end of the activity, evaluate which chart or recording technique was the most effective and efficient. With long term activities, such as Waste Not; Want Not, and A Sign of the Times, be sure to allocate additional pages to record observations.

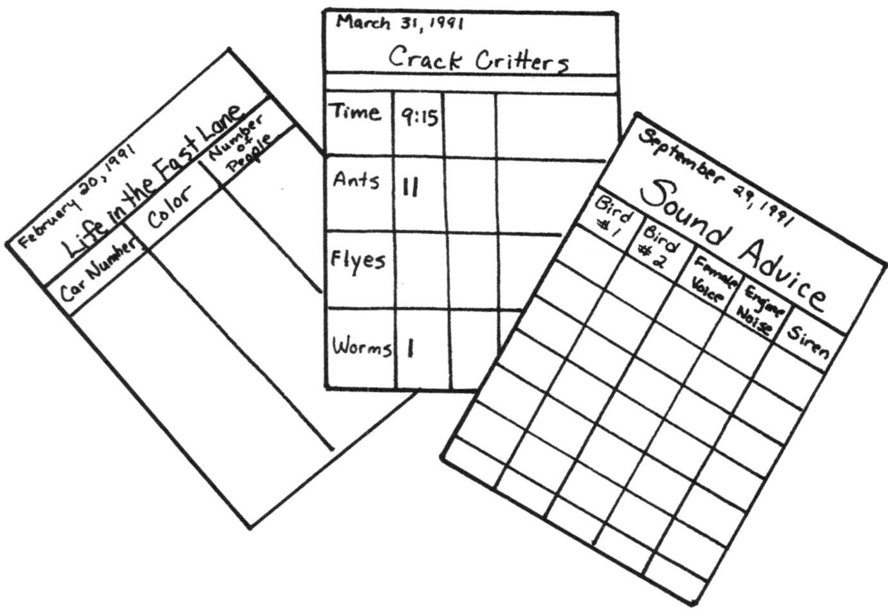

Simple graphs can be constructed and included right in the Observation Book. Bar graphs are easily constructed and reveal meaningful trends ("Hot Colors"). Once again, you may want to set a standard for the first one or two that the class includes.

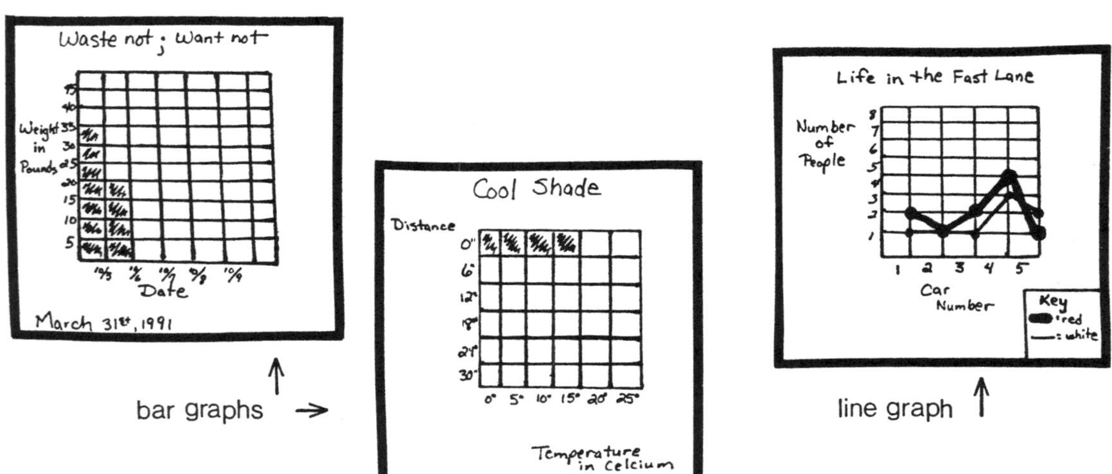

Before any data collecting is started, the type of data should be listed. This will help in the design of a chart as well as remind students what type of information they are seeking. Caution: Do not attempt to include too much in the individual Observation Books. Combining all teams' results into a chart or graph should be encouraged, but class charts and graphs are more effective when constructed as a separate activity.

Recording Data Outdoors

When using the Observation Book outside, it will be necessary to provide a "clipboard." Glue or staple two pieces of corrugated cardboard together. This will provide support and protection from the damp ground. Use two rubber bands to hold the Observation Book in place on the cardboard. Students can easily make these "clipboards" for themselves, adding their own personalization.

Storage of Observation Books

You may want to assign a special area, box, or crate for storing the individual Observation Books. We all know that a student's desk is not the ideal location for a small, paperbound book! At the end of the school year, each book will serve as a valuable record of the year's scientific investigations. Make your own Observation Book to provide a basis of comparison for the next year. Each year, build on the information included. In no time, a valuable resource book will have been created!

Earth Science Activities

Dewdrops

Earth's atmosphere recycles 1 trillion tons of water per day. It seems impossible that so much water can be recycled without being noticed. This activity helps your classroom ecologists see the "hydrologic cycle" in action on a small scale. The results can then be applied to the larger, worldwide "rain machine."

Relevance to Everyday Life

Moisture is necessary for every living thing, but city dwellers often overlook the source. What practical application does dew (moisture in the air) have for the ecology of the city? Is the water in dew enough to matter? Who would, or could, use this source of water? Where does dew come from?

Materials

- ☐ Plastic wrap—Approximately 6" x 6"
- ☐ Plastic glass or jar
- ☐ Stones
- ☐ Rubber band
- ☐ Small scale
- ☐ Absorbent paper towels of known size and mass (optional)
- ☐ Observation Books
- ☐ Pencils

How to Do It

Put the rocks in the bottom of the cup for weight. Place the plastic wrap over the plastic cup. The plastic wrap should form a shallow bowl over the opening of the glass. Use a rubber band to hold the plastic wrap in place. Have each team choose a location outside where they think they might collect the most dew. At the end of the school day, place the containers in the chosen positions. Record the positions in the Observation Books. Leave the containers in place overnight. (If it rains, you will need to start the experiment again.)

Data Collecting and Recording

Upon arriving in the morning, collect the containers. Without spilling any dew, carefully fold the edges of the plastic wrap to form a little bag that will hold the water. Use the rubber band to hold the bag shut until the investigative team is ready to measure the water.

If a scale is not available, pour the water out onto a paper towel and measure the wet area. Measure by finding the area of a circle ($A=\pi r^2$), or use a piece of quadrille paper and count the squares (see the Appendix), or cut the wet circle out of the paper towel when it has stopped spreading and compare circle sizes among teams. Graph team results weekly for an ongoing study.

Extension Activities

- Correlate the dew collected with the atmospheric conditions of the day, especially the percent humidity (use a hygrometer, a sling psychrometer, or consult your local weather service for the day's humidity).
- Calculate how much dew collects in the school block on a given night.
- Repeat the activity using a variety of collecting surfaces. Is there a difference in the amount of dew collected?

Name ______________________

Lab 1 Dewdrops

Team ______________________ Date ____________

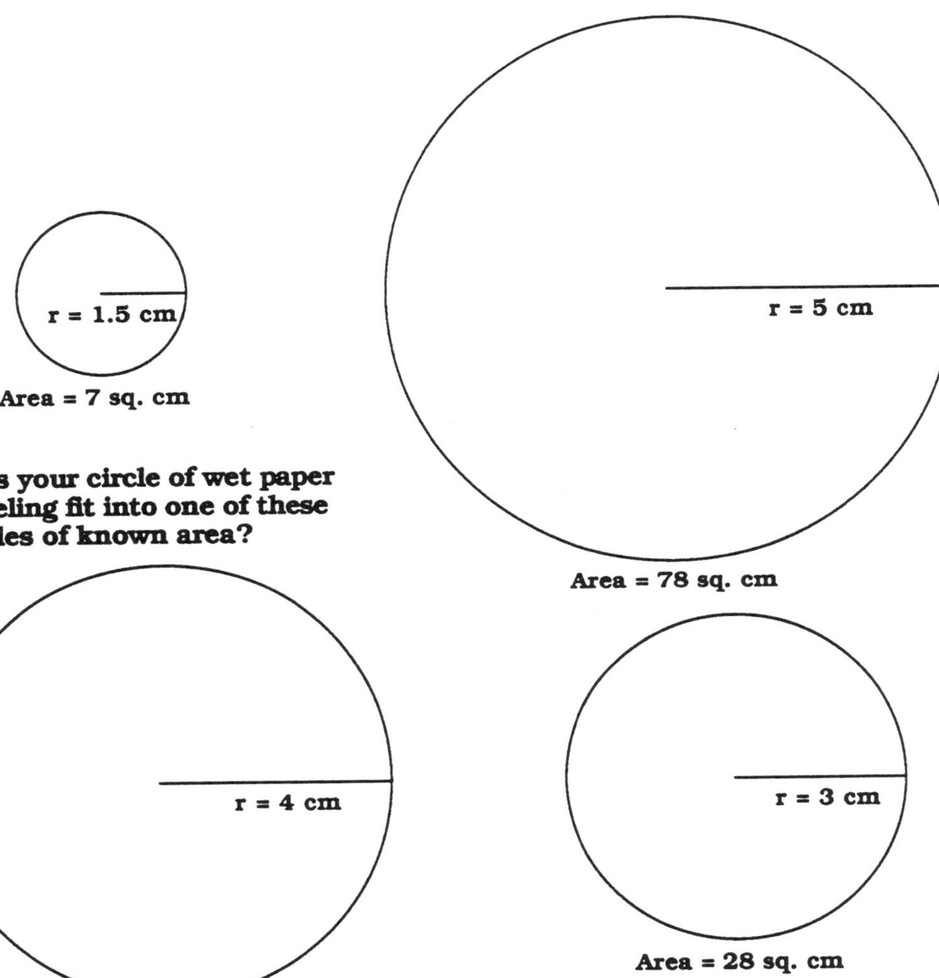

If your paper towel circle does not fit any of these circles, measure the radius (*r*) of your circle of wet paper.

____ x ____ x 3.14 = ____
r   *r*   π   *Area*

Second Method:

Lay your cut-out circle of wet paper on a piece of quadrille paper. Count the number of squares covered or touched by the circle.

Number of squares = ____

Name ______________________________

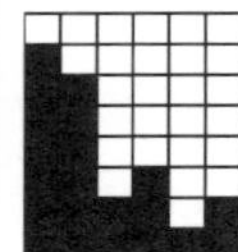

Dewdrops

Date ________________

Class Dew Collection

Duplicate this sheet for each time dew will be collected.

NUMBER OF TEAMS								
16								
15								
14								
13								
12								
11								
10								
9								
8								
7								
6								
5								
4								
3								
2								
1								

AREA

If you used the formula $Area = \pi r^2$, label the x-axis with square inches or centimeters. An example might be 0.5 square inch, 1.0 square inch, 1.5 square inches, and so forth across the axis.

If you used quadrille paper to calculate area, label the x-axis with the number of squares that were covered by the paper toweling. An example might be 10 squares, 20 squares, 30 squares, and so forth across the axis.

A Sign of the Times

Shadows change with the time of day and the season. To many forms of life, this is an important indicator of seasonal cycles. Students will analyze shadow changes over several months and relate the changes to seasons, cycles, and Earth's position.

Relevance to Everyday Life

All systems on Earth are run by the cyclical clock, which is based upon light duration and intensity. This investigation allows students to see that shadows can be used to predict cycles (time and season), and suggests that plants and animals use this information as well.

Materials

- ☐ Measuring stick or tape
- ☐ Observation Books
- ☐ Pencils

How to Do It

Have each team of students adopt a "shadow maker" such as a flagpole, tree, telephone pole or light post. If there are not enough shadow makers, use the measuring sticks at specific, predetermined spots. The recording of the exact location is critical as this activity should be repeated throughout the year. Determine the day(s) of the month on which your class will take its readings. Make one reading in the morning and one in the afternoon on the chosen dates.

Data Collecting and Recording

Each team should have a separate page for each recording with a sketch of the shadow maker and its shadow length drawn to scale. Be sure to make all recordings on standard time, not daylight savings time! Keep the notebooks uniform, in fact, you might have the teams prepare all the recording pages in advance by tracing the drawing of the shadow maker (no shadow) from the first one. There should be a separate page for each time of the day as well as for each day. Be sure that the exact measurement is recorded and converted to the appropriate scale.

Extension Activities

- You may consider keeping two notebooks, one for the morning and one for the afternoon. If the booklets are approximately 5" x 7", they can be held in one hand while the other hand flips the pages quickly, causing an illusion of movement (the "flip book" idea).
- Have teams compare shadow length and position change. Does the location of the shadow maker affect the results? Create a class graph with the *x*-axis representing the object length and the *y*-axis representing the shadow length.

Name ___________________________

A Sign of the Times

Team ___________________________ Date ______________

Location of shadow maker ___________________________

____

Draw your shadow maker (examples: flagpole, tree, telephone pole, light post). Then draw the shadow it makes.

Duplicate this sheet for each day shadows will be recorded.

N

AM Drawing

Date ____________ Time __________

PM Drawing

Date ____________ Time __________

W

E

S

Deep Freeze

How deep does the snow get in your schoolyard? How deep does it get in other areas of the nation? How is the wildlife affected? As students measure snow depth on the schoolyard, they will try to answer these questions.

Relevance to Everyday Life

Snowfall provides water, insulation, and cover for animals and plants. Does snowfall alter the water table as much as rainfall does? What plants and animals benefit most from snowfalls in your city?

Materials

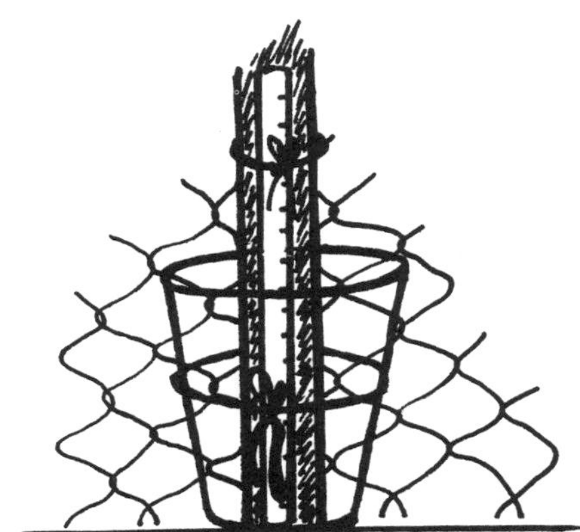

- ☐ Rulers, or sticks with calibrations for measuring
- ☐ Plastic cup or jar
- ☐ String or rope
- ☐ Observation Books
- ☐ Pencils

How to Do It

Before a snowfall, place a ruler in an open jar or cup. Tie the cup to a pole in an open area near the school.

Data Collection and Recording

After the snowfall, read the ruler to determine the amount of snow that has fallen. Compare the results with other teams. Are they the same?

Extension Activities

- Take the jar of snow indoors after reading the depth. Allow the snow to melt. Compare the depth of the melted snow to the snow level. Calculate the percent of loss space (subtract the water level from the snowfall level). Measure the pH level. Is it the same as rain water? Tap water?
- Make a snowfall map of your schoolyard. Be sure to include a legend!
- Measure each snowfall. Make a chart to record snowfall by month. Which month has the most snow? Compare your measurements to data from your local weather bureau.

Name ______________________________

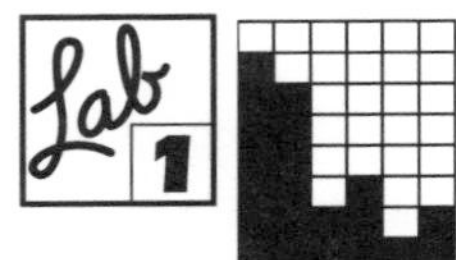

Deep Freeze

Date ______________

Class Graph

Duplicate this graph for each day, week or month that snowfall will be collected.

NUMBER OF TEAMS

16										
15										
14										
13										
12										
11										
10										
9										
8										
7										
6										
5										
4										
3										
2										
1										
	1 inch	**2 inch**	**3 inch**	**4 inch**	**5 inch**	**6 inch**	**7 inch**	**8 inch**	**9 inch**	**10 inch**

AMOUNT OF SNOWFALL

Amount of Melted Snow *

*Use another color on your graph to show the depth of the "melted snow." Compare the bars. Which depth is greater, the snow or the melted snow? Does one particular depth (3 inches, for example) of snowfall always give the same depth of melted snow?

Geological Glances

Humans use a great number of resources from Earth to construct buildings. How many different examples of these Earth products can be found on a scavenger hunt of the school grounds?

Relevance to Everyday Life

Deforestation, strip mining, and draining of wetlands occur at an alarming rate to provide the land and buildings that are in demand today. Discuss this use of natural resources and the effects it has on the ecosystem. What changes can be made?

Materials

- ☐ Crayon with paper removed
- ☐ Plain paper, such as newsprint, for rubbings
- ☐ Penny
- ☐ Nail
- ☐ Glass bottle
- ☐ Observation Books
- ☐ Pencils

How to Do It

Have teams search the school grounds for building materials. Observe brick or concrete facing material, shutters, windows, doors, sidewalks, rooftops.

Data Collecting and Recording

Have students make rubbings of as many surfaces as possible. Record the colors. Use Moh's Scale of Hardness to determine the hardness of the surface (fingernail scratches surface = 2.5; penny = 3; nail = 6.5; surface scratches glass bottle = 7). Create a class chart of the Earth materials recorded. Attempt to find out where the original materials came from and how much of structure is covered by the material (1/2, all, 1/3, 75%).

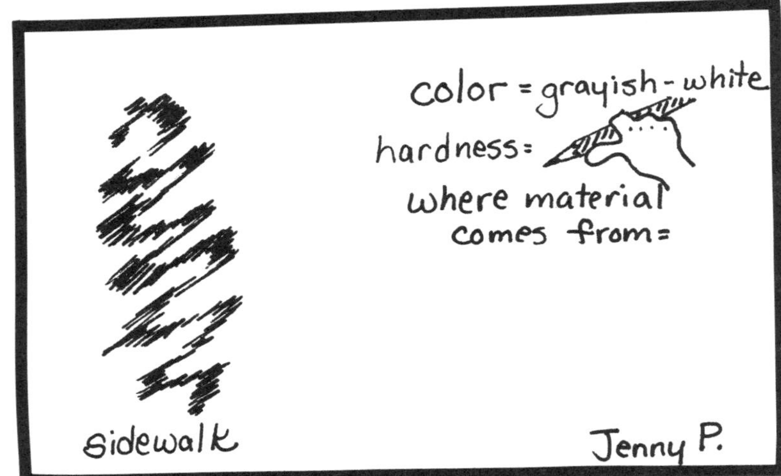

Extension Activities

- Invite a builder or developer to the class so students can ask questions. Ask the builder to be prepared with facts and figures on the amount of materials needed to construct a 2- or 3-story building. Estimate the number of buildings in the city and the total amount of Earth material used.
- What other materials could be used in construction? Have students use their imaginations to design a "building of the future" as a group. Build a scale model.

Name ______________________

Geological Glances

Team ______________________ Date ______________

Look for different building materials (such as glass, brick, concrete) outside. Make a rubbing of the different building materials you find. Identify the type of material, color, and hardness of each.

Material ________ **Color** ________ **Hardness** ______	**Material** ________ **Color** ________ **Hardness** ______	**Material** ________ **Color** ________ **Hardness** ______
Material ________ **Color** ________ **Hardness** ______	**Material** ________ **Color** ________ **Hardness** ______	**Material** ________ **Color** ________ **Hardness** ______
Material ________ **Color** ________ **Hardness** ______	**Material** ________ **Color** ________ **Hardness** ______	**Material** ________ **Color** ________ **Hardness** ______

Lab 1 Geological Glances

Name ______________________

Date ____________

Class Chart of Geological Building Materials

BUILDING MATERIALS								
MATERIAL	Concrete	Brick	Blacktop	Wood	Metal	Glass	Shingle	*
COLOR								
HARDNESS (from Moh's scale)								
ORIGIN (where it came from in Earth)								
AMOUNT OF BUILDING COVERED (give % or fraction)								
EXAMPLES OF WHERE FOUND								

*Add your own column title for building materials you discover that are not on this chart!

Cool Shade

Shady areas help to create uneven heating. Air currents are created and move from one place to another. Is shade in one area as cool as shade in another area? Does the type of shade make a difference? Have your students use their thermometers to investigate!

Relevance to Everyday Life

Rising columns of hot air from the Earth are replaced by cooler air rushing in to fill the space. Have students speculate on the source of this cooler air. Discuss air convection currents and the practical uses of such currents. Although students will think of hot air balloons, gliders, and hang gliders, help them to see the application to birds that soar, such as eagles and vultures. Soaring birds not only ride the currents, but they also rely on the rising columns of air to deliver the scents of their next meal. Wind and weather patterns also depend on the phenomenon, which contributes to the climatic patterns of the world. With the decline of the trees in the rainforests, climatic patterns are changing worldwide (trees create temperature variations).

Materials

- ☐ Thermometer
- ☐ Observation Books
- ☐ Pencils
- ☐ Streamer
- ☐ Stick
- ☐ Tape

How to Do It

Assign areas of shade to each team of students. It may be necessary to use shadows cast by poles and buildings in order to have enough areas for each team. Decide upon a certain hour of the day when you will take these temperatures, and always try to record temperatures at that time.

Data Collecting and Recording

Have students take temperatures at a specified distance from the object making the shadow so that heat from the object is not influencing the reading. Since this will be done on a sunny day, it is a good idea to take a temperature reading in the sunlight for comparison.

Make an easy "wind measurer"! Attach a six-inch piece of streamer to a stick. Ask students to observe breezes in both sunny and shady areas.

Shade graphs should be made by each team. Make a master *Shady Spots* graph for the entire class.

Extension Activities

- Does distance from the "shade maker" influence the temperature reading? Have students take the temperature every six inches from the shade maker until the effect is not noticed. This could lead into a study on heat capacity, or on insulation.
- Find an inexpensive radiometer (check with your local middle or high school). Place it in the shade and then move it into the sunlight. How does the effect of hot air rising make the radiometer work?

Name ______________________

Lab 1

Cool Shade

Team ______________________ Date ____________

Time Taken ____________

Be sure to use a different color for each location. Include a legend!

TEMPERATURE

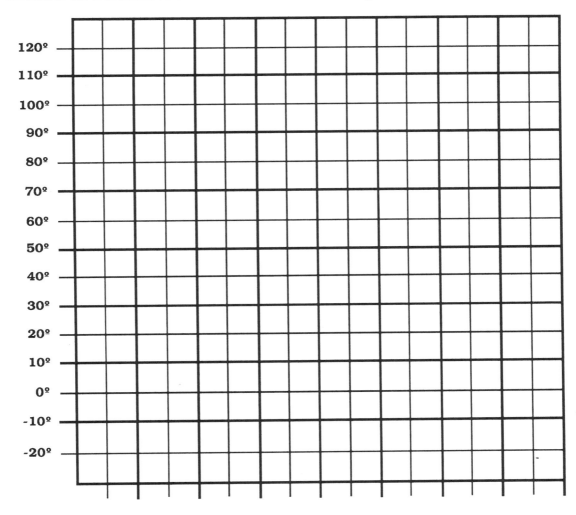

120º
110º
100º
90º
80º
70º
60º
50º
40º
30º
20º
10º
0º
-10º
-20º

DATE

Sunny Temperature = _____

Don't forget to label the dates for which you recorded temperatures on the x-axis.

Name ______________________________

Cool Shade

Date ______________

Shady Spots—Class Graph (For individual day recording)

Duplicate this page for each day temperatures will be collected.

TEMPERATURE						
120º						
110º						
100º						
90º						
80º						
70º						
60º						
50º						
40º						
30º						
20º						
10º						
0º						
-10º						
-20º						
	Location I (Team I)	Location II (Team II)	Location III (Team III)	Location IV (Team IV)	Location V (Team V)	Location VI (Team VI)

LOCATIONS

Name ________________________________

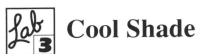

Cool Shade

Team ________________________________ Date ______________

Date started ______________

Shady Spots—Class Graph (For consecutive recording days)

Use a different-colored marker for each team. Make a legend to identify each team's color.

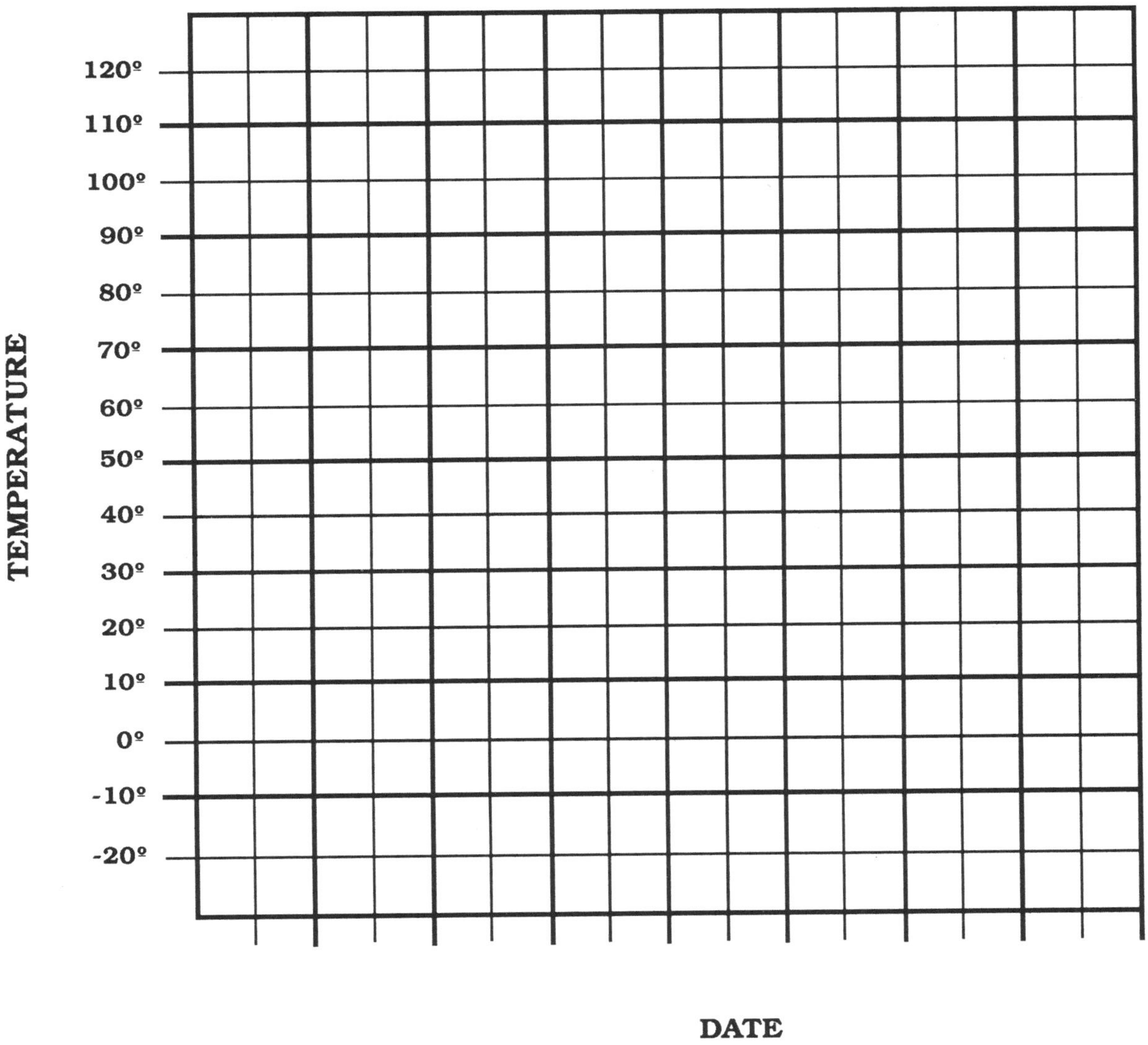

TEMPERATURE

120º
110º
100º
90º
80º
70º
60º
50º
40º
30º
20º
10º
0º
-10º
-20º

DATE

Don't forget to label the dates for which you recorded temperatures on the *x*-axis.

It's the Same Everywhere You Go

Turn a rainy school day into an exciting study of rainfall. Combine science and math as students collect, measure, and compare the rainfall at various locations on the school property.

Relevance to Everyday Life

In landscaping, it is critical that plants be placed in locations that ensure optimal growth. Some locations receive little rainfall because they are sheltered by a building, or other vegetation. Other locations get too much water from rain because of the run-off from a nearby roof.

Materials

- ☐ Empty glass soda pop bottle (Note: all teams must have identical bottles)
- ☐ Ruler
- ☐ Funnel
- ☐ Clay
- ☐ Small wooden dowel
- ☐ Observation Books
- ☐ Pencils

How to Do It

Place a small amount of clay around the top of the soda pop bottle. Set the funnel on the top, pressing down firmly so that a seal is formed between the funnel and the bottle. Each field team should select a location to place their rain collector, and note the surrounding conditions. (Is there shade? Is it protected? In which direction is the building?) Encourage collection at a variety of locations, such as near the building, under a tree, and out in the open, so that comparisons can be made. If it is windy, or if there is a chance the bottle will get tipped over, secure it by tying it to an object (such as a fence post or tree), or by building up the earth around it.

Data Collecting and Recording

At the end of the day, gather the rain collectors. Stick a small dowel into the bottle until it touches the bottom. Remove the dowel and measure the water line with a ruler, just as you measure oil in a car with a dipstick. Be sure that the bottom of the ruler is even with the end of the dowel. Record the amount of water on a chart. Compare your results with those from other rain collectors. Did all rain collectors contain the same amount of rainfall? Repeat this investigation on other days. Do the results stay the same? Does the season make a difference?

Extension Activities

- Make a map of the school property. Color-code the map according to the amount of rainfall.
- Make a monthly and yearly rainfall chart. Compare it to the National Weather Bureau's statistics. Your local newspaper or a national newspaper such as *USA Today* should have the necessary statistics.
- Make a rain collector for use at home. Compare the results to the information collected at school.
- If you are in a location that receives snow, compare snowfall amounts. See the activity Deep Freeze.

Name ____________________

It's the Same Everywhere You Go

Team ____________________ Date ____________

Fill in this chart with all the information gathered by your class.

Team	Location of Rain Collector	Amount of Water

Don't forget to include the unit of measure you used in determining the amount of water in the rain collector!

Fading Away

The rays of the sun not only make Earth suitable for life, they also can be destructive. In this activity, students will see how sunlight affects construction paper.

Relevance to Everyday Life

In states where the sun's rays can be intense, windows are often treated with solar film that reflects the light. Daily exposure to strong sunlight can cause carpeting, car upholstery, and furniture to fade. What colors seem to be affected the most? When looking at car interiors, which will show the least damage?

Materials

- [ ] Six sheets of construction paper, same color
- [ ] Various objects to set on the paper (*Suggestions include a washer, rock, pencil, shell, twig, coin.*)
- [ ] Observation Books
- [ ] Pencils

How to Do It

In the morning have each investigative team choose a color of construction paper. Each team will need six pieces of the same color paper. Color, as well as intensity of color, should vary among the teams. Label each piece of paper as follows. Label the control sheet (the one that is never in the sun) *Control*. The remaining five pieces should be labeled from *1* to *5*. The number represents how many days the paper will be exposed to sunlight. Students should choose a location for their construction paper that receives sunlight throughout the entire day. The construction paper may need to be secured to the ground by placing a rock at each corner. Arrange various other objects on the paper.

Data Collecting and Recording

To limit the number of variables, investigative teams should place the same objects on each piece of paper. Tape the objects in place with transparent tape. After 5 hours, which color shows the most "sun damage" by fading? Can the image of the object be clearly seen on the construction paper? Set the papers numbered *2* to *5* in the sunlight a second day. Are the results the same? Set the papers numbered *3* to *5* in the sunlight a third day. Is there any difference? Repeat for day four and day five. Compare the results after the fifth day. Be sure to include pieces of the construction paper from each day in your Observation Book.

Extension Activities

- Contact a local car dealership. What color interior is the most popular? Second most popular? Third? How does the most popular color compare with the color that fades the most?
- Set up the same experiment, but this time place a piece of solar film over the construction paper. Compare the results.
- Combine this investigation with the activity Hot Colors. What correlation is there between temperature and fading?

Name ______________________

Lab 1 Fading Away

Team ______________________ Date started ______________

Control	1 Day	2 Days
3 Days	**4 Days**	**5 Days**

Color that faded the most in 5 days: ______________

Color that faded the least in 5 days: ______________

Environmental Activities

Litter Bugs

Natural litter plays a very important role in the ecosystem. Many organisms are dependent on the litter. Students will become detectives as they search through natural litter in an attempt to find clues that critters were there. Perhaps a few detectives will even be lucky enough to discover the actual critters!

Relevance to Everyday Life

Every organism on Earth plays a vital role in keeping nature in balance. It's easy to overlook little critters that act as recyclers, breaking down material and returning it to the soil. This activity also shows how adaptable organisms can be.

Materials

- ☐ Cardboard drink container—individual-serving size
- ☐ Paper cup
- ☐ Magnifying glass
- ☐ Observation Books
- ☐ Pencils

How to Do It

Have each team scoop up a containerful of leaf litter from the ground. Shake it gently so that any critters in the container will settle to the bottom. Remove the leaf litter carefully, looking for critters as it is emptied. When a critter is found, place it in the paper cup for closer inspection. Repeat this several times.

Data Collecting and Recording

As the critters are collected, sketch each one in the Observation Books. Students should note the number of legs, antennae, wings, and coloring. If more than one of a particular critter is found, record the number. Compare the results from all teams and create a graph representing the numbers found.

Extension Activities

- What is the average size of the critters found? Does there seem to be a maximum size? A minimum?
- What area of the schoolyard had the most evidence of critters? Why? Repeat the activity in one month. Are the results the same?
- Compare the number and size of critters found in natural litter to that of human-made litter. Is there a difference?

Name ______________________________

Lab 1 Litter Bugs

Team ______________________________ Date ______________

What critter can you find in nature's litter? Use this chart to record information on each critter you find. Duplicate this page for each day of collecting.

CRITTER SHAPES

	CRITTER #1	CRITTER #2	CRITTER #3	CRITTER #4
Number of legs				
Shape of antenna (draw)				
Wing shape (sketch)				
Color				
Size (measure in mm)				
Number found				
Top view sketch				

Name ______________________________

Litter Bugs

Team ______________________________ Date ______________

Critter Count–Class Bar Graph

Duplicate this graph for each day of collecting.

NUMBER OF CRITTERS

16								
15								
14								
13								
12								
11								
10								
9								
8								
7								
6								
5								
4								
3								
2								
1								
	Type A	**Type B**	**Type C**	**Type D**	**Type E**	**Type F**	**Type G**	**Type H**

TYPE OF CRITTER FOUND

Critter Types

Type A = 6 legs, antennae, wings
Type B = 6 legs, antennae, no wings
Type C = 6 legs, no antennae, no wings
Type D = 8 legs, antennae, wings
Type E = 8 legs, no antennae, no wings
Type F = 10 legs

* Add your own categories!

Quality Control

How does the air quality on the school grounds compare with that at the street corner one block away? In this investigation, students will trap particles in the air to see if there is a difference in the air that is part of their environment.

Relevance to Everyday Life

There are two kinds of air pollution: gases and solid particles. Solid particles come from nature (dust or pollen), and from humans (car exhaust, smoke stacks of factories). Since the air enters our bodies through our respiratory system, it is important to know if the air we breathe is clean. If it is not, steps need to be taken to clean the air.

Materials

- ☐ Cardboard—10 cm square
- ☐ String—20 inches long
- ☐ Clear adhesive paper, such as contact paper (to cover cardboard)
- ☐ Thumbtacks—20
- ☐ Permanent marker
- ☐ Ruler
- ☐ Strong magnifier or microscope
- ☐ Observation Books
- ☐ Pencils

How to Do It

Thread the string through two adjacent corners of the cardboard so that it can hang. Rule off the cardboard into 1-centimeter squares using the ruler and a dark, permanent marker. Cover this ruled surface with the clear adhesive paper, sticky side out. Hold the edges in place with the thumbtacks, placed every 2 centimeters. Suspend the pollution collectors in prearranged locations around the school, both inside and outside. Also try to hang some near a busy intersection and a factory.

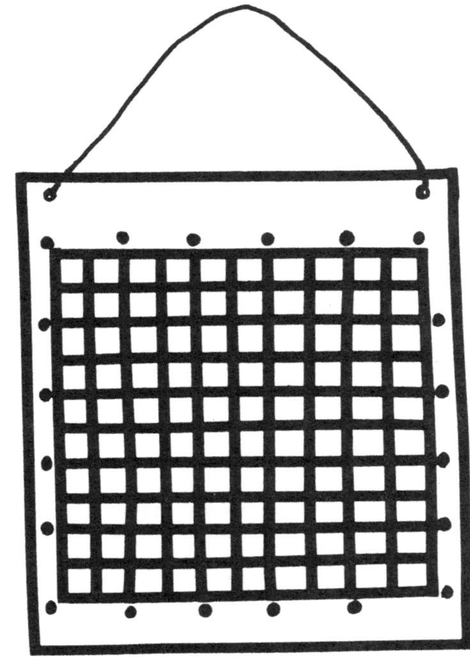

Data Collecting and Recording

After 5 days, collect all the pollution collectors. Be sure to mark the location of each collector! Choose about 10 squares that are representative of the pollution collector. Find the average for the collector (add the total number of particles in the representative squares and then divide by 10). Compare locations. Which collector had the most trapped particles? Why? Use a strong magnifier to look at the solid particles. Draw some of the different particles that were trapped.

Extension Activities

- Using a strong magnifier, identify the particles collected on the pollution collector. Try to trace their origin (burning trash, industrial release, pollen, natural litter—such as leaf bits).
- Repeat the investigation and include other areas of the city.
- If your city keeps a daily pollution index, graph it over a month or over the school year. Which months are worse? Why?

Name ____________________

Lab 1 Quality Control

Team ____________________ Date ____________

Location of Collector: ____________________

Our Results

Square Number	Number of Particles
1	
2	
3	
4	
5	
6	
7	
8	
9	
10	
Total	

To find the average for the collector (fill in the blanks): ______ (Total number of particles) ÷ 10 (Number of squares counted) = ______ (Average number of particles)

Class Results

Team	Location	Average # of Particles

Here is how some of our particles looked:

Life in the Fast Lane

When asked what a car pool was, Jenny replied that it was a pool inside a car. Jenny's concept of *pool* was a body of water, not a collection of people. In this activity, students will observe and record the number of cars containing more than one person that go by their school.

Relevance to Everyday Life

One way to reduce the consumption of our natural resources is to carpool. Modern freeways often contain car pool lanes, open only to cars with two or more people. How does the number of "carpoolers" in your school area rate?

Materials

- ☐ Observation Books
- ☐ Pencils

How to Do It

Investigative teams should position themselves near the street(s) by their school. **Teams must be a safe distance from the street! Sitting or standing on curbs is not safe!!** Set a time limit of 10 minutes for the observation period.

Data Collecting and Recording

In a team of two, one student is responsible for stating the color of car and the number of people inside, and the second student is responsible for recording the data. Car color and number of people should be recorded together. Each team records only traffic flowing in one direction on the street. Multiple teams recording the same data improves accuracy. What percentage of the cars had multiple riders? Go out again at a different time of day (be sure to stand in the same spot). Are the results the same?

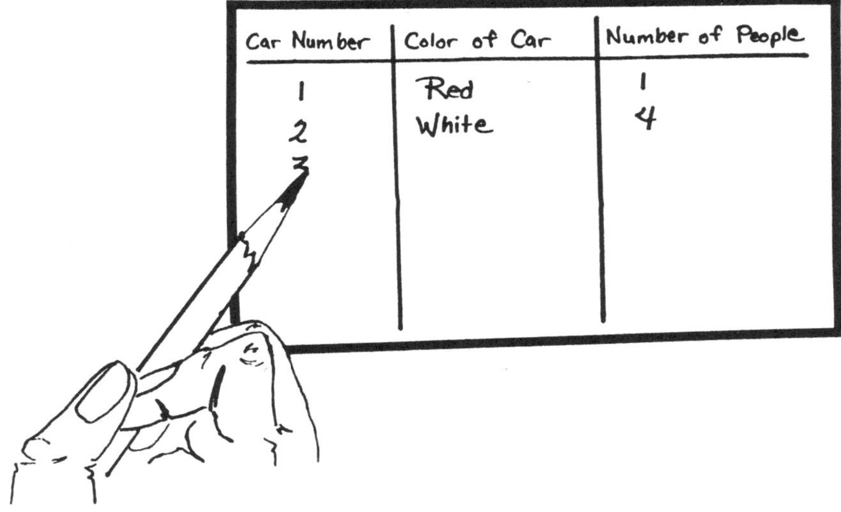

Car Number
Color of Car
Number of People
1
Red
1
2
White
4
3

Extension Activities

- Results can be graphed by car color. Does one color seem to stand out as a "car pool color?" Why or why not?
- Write a letter to the editor of your local paper encouraging the use of car pools.
- Try to increase the use of car pools among students. Can students form car pools for transportation to school and other events?
- Repeat the activity. This time record the make of cars that pass as well as the number of occupants. Research and report the gas mileage for city driving of each car. Is there any correlation between the gas mileage and the number of passengers?

Name ______________________________

Life in the Fast Lane

Team ______________________________ Date ______________

Location ______________________________ Time ______________

Record all the cars traveling in the same direction. Watch carefully! Some cars go fast!

Car Color	Number of Occupants

Car Color	Number of Occupants

Name ______________________________

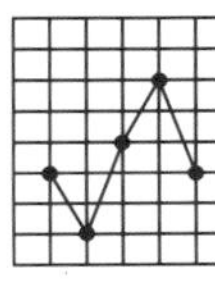

Life in the Fast Lane

Team ______________________________ Date ______________

Location ______________________________ Time ______________

LEGEND

Car Color	Color on Graph

Nature's Paintbox

We have heard the phrase, "all the colors of the rainbow." Are all the colors present in nature? Which colors are more prominent in the city? Why? Send students outside sleuthing as they try to find the answers!

Relevance to Everyday Life

Colors occur in nature as a result of light variation and pigment content. Over the course of the year, prominent colors change. How does a plant or animal use nature's colors to its advantage?

Materials

- ☐ Color charts or paint chip samples (a local hardware store will usually supply these on request)
- ☐ Observation Books
- ☐ Pencils

How to Do It

Decide upon a specific area for each team to investigate. Have teams search the immediate school area for naturally occurring colors. Human-made products cannot be used. Count the number of occurrences of each color. When fall arrives, you might revise the count by gathering a small bag of leaves at random and counting the colors contained in the specified area.

Data Collecting and Recording

Make a class chart for the colors that are found and the number of occurrences. Label it for the current month. Data should be charted so it resembles a graph with the colors at the bottom (the x-axis) and the frequencies along the side (y-axis). Ideally there should be one class chart for each month of the school year so that comparisons can be made. Charts could be hung along the wall.

Extension Activities

- Practice working with percent. Convert the frequency of each color (number of occurrences in an area) to percent of the total colors found. How does it vary throughout the year?
- Gather the same kind of data from other areas of the city. Are the results the same? Plan a field trip to "the country". Is the frequency of color the same? Why or why not?

Name ______________________________

Nature's Paintbox

Team ______________________________ Date ______________

Can you find all the colors of the rainbow outside your school? Use this graph to record your findings. Make one copy of this graph for each month of the school year.

NUMBER OF TIMES A PIGMENT OCCURS

16								
15								
14								
13								
12								
11								
10								
9								
8								
7								
6								
5								
4								
3								
2								
1								

PIGMENTS

Don't forget! The *x*-axis is for the colors you find. Attach samples of each color to the graph. You may also write the name of the color between the lines.

Waste Not; Want Not!

What better place to practice conservation than in your school cafeteria? Can students reduce the amount of garbage generated during lunch? Give it a try and see!

Relevance to Everyday Life

As a society, we generate a lot of trash. Landfills are rapidly becoming full and closing, leaving communities scrambling to find other places to dispose of their refuse. Products claiming to be biodegradable are showing up on supermarket shelves, only to be proven not to decompose. The answer lies not only in recycling products, but in cutting back on our waste. Can your students meet the challenge, starting in the school cafeteria?

Materials

- [ ] Garbage bags of trash from the cafeteria
- [ ] Scale
- [ ] Observation Books
- [ ] Pencils

How to Do It

Without any prior announcement, bring the filled and sealed cafeteria garbage containers to your classroom. CAUTION: Advise children not to handle items in the trash. Weigh the individual garbage bags. Add the individual weights together to get a total for the day. Discuss how landfills in the country are becoming full. What would happen if there was no place to take this garbage? What steps could the students take to decrease the amount of garbage generated? Some suggestions may include: eating all the food on the trays; bringing lunch in lunch boxes or cloth bags; using containers to hold food instead of plastic bags that must be thrown away; using cloth napkins; or using thermos bottles instead of juice boxes or milk cartons.

Data Collecting and Recording

Decide how often the garbage will be weighed. Put a calendar in the Observation Books. Record the weight of the garbage on the calendar. On the specified days, weigh the garbage and record the outcome on the calendar. Compare the results. Is the amount of garbage decreasing? Does the meal offered in the cafeteria affect the results?

Extension Activities

- Alert the entire school to the project and encourage their participation. Make a giant graph to display in the cafeteria. With the whole school working together, is the amount of garbage decreased?
- Expand the project to include the trash generated in each classroom. Which class is able to decrease their garbage the most?

(continued on page 33)

- Have students keep track of everything they throw away at school for a week. After analyzing the refuse, have teams decide which items could be kept and recycled. The way the product is reused may be very different from its original purpose. For the next week, have students categorize the refuse and separate it into the appropriate category.
- Calculate the percent of refuse which would not need to be taken to a landfill or an incinerator. If each American discards approximately 3.5 pounds per day, determine how much refuse it would be in one year? How much for the entire population of the United States?

Name ____________________

Waste Not; Want Not

Team ____________________ Date ____________

Month of ____________				
Monday	**Tuesday**	**Wednesday**	**Thursday**	**Friday**

Be sure to include the date, menu and weight of the garbage on the calendar!

Name ______________________________

Waste Not; Want Not

Class ______________________________ Date ______________

Use the *x*-axis to record the dates on which you weighed the garbage.

Amount of Garbage in Pounds

34 lb.								
32 lb.								
30 lb.								
28 lb.								
26 lb.								
24 lb.								
22 lb.								
20 lb.								
18 lb.								
16 lb.								
14 lb.								
12 lb.								
10 lb.								
8 lb.								
6 lb.								
4 lb.								
2 lb.								

Date

Don't forget to give your graph a title!

Plot Sleuths

The area around a schoolyard undergoes change. Is the change due to natural causes, or the surroundings? As students investigate the clues, they will develop the basic process skills of observation, inference, classification, measurement, and prediction.

Relevance to Everyday Life

Undeveloped or abandoned areas in urban settings often undergo changes called "succession," which are typical of natural ecosystems. Cracked sidewalks may reveal plant growth, decaying buildings resemble rotting logs, and crumbling buildings can be compared to eroding mountains. Succession, simply stated, means that one form of life becomes more successful and dominant than the one preceding it. Environmental, as well as physical, causes may precipitate this change. How fast does it occur? What is responsible for the change? Are the changes good or undesirable? How can they be prevented or encouraged?

Materials

- ☐ String, 10 feet long
- ☐ Observation Books
- ☐ Pencils

How to Do It

Choose an outdoor area to be studied. It can be a weedy patch or part of the blacktop or cemented area. Allow each team to choose a specific area to lay out the plot. Plots should not overlap! Careful measurements must be made so that the plot can be found easily throughout the school year. Measure specific distances from the corner of the building, a tree, a parking lot, or other semipermanent landmark.

Using the 10-foot string, plot out a square (10 feet to a side) to study. Mark the corners with craft or Popsicle sticks. Examine the interior of the plot carefully for life forms, cracks, exposed earth, stones, sticks, anything!

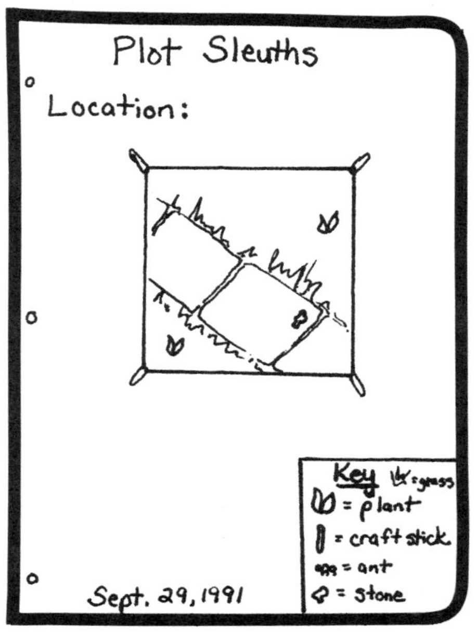

Data Collecting and Recording

Draw the plot in the Observation Book along with the exact distance from the reference point. DO NOT RELY ON MEMORY. Everything within the plot should be sketched, including grasses, weeds, flowers, stones, litter, or cracks. Be sure to include a key to the illustrations. Do any interrelationships exist between what you find there? If so, list the relationships. Predict future relationships or changes you anticipate. Plan to visit the plot site each month to observe changes. Which changes were caused by nature? Which were caused by humans?

Extension Activities

- Find a plot near your home that is different from the one at school. Mark it off and record monthly changes on the plot. Compare it to the plot at school.

(continued on page 37)

- Plan methods you could use to prevent succession (change) on the plots you are studying. Plan methods you could use to encourage succession on the plots. Test out your hypotheses.
- Are there any "natural areas" in your community which are currently undergoing succession? Are they natural or human-caused forms of succession?
- Find out if your community has a "Land Use Plan" that includes open areas where natural succession can take place. If not, draft a letter to your local government officials requesting that open areas be left natural.

Name ______________________

Plot Sleuths

Team ______________________ Date ____________

10 '

10 ' 10 '

10 '

Key

Sketch your plot. Duplicate this page for each time the plot will be visited.
Finding the plot (specific distances from reference points, such as the flagpole, the corner of the building, or the fence):

____

____

____

____

Don't forget to label North, South, East, and West on your plot sketch!

Life Science Activities

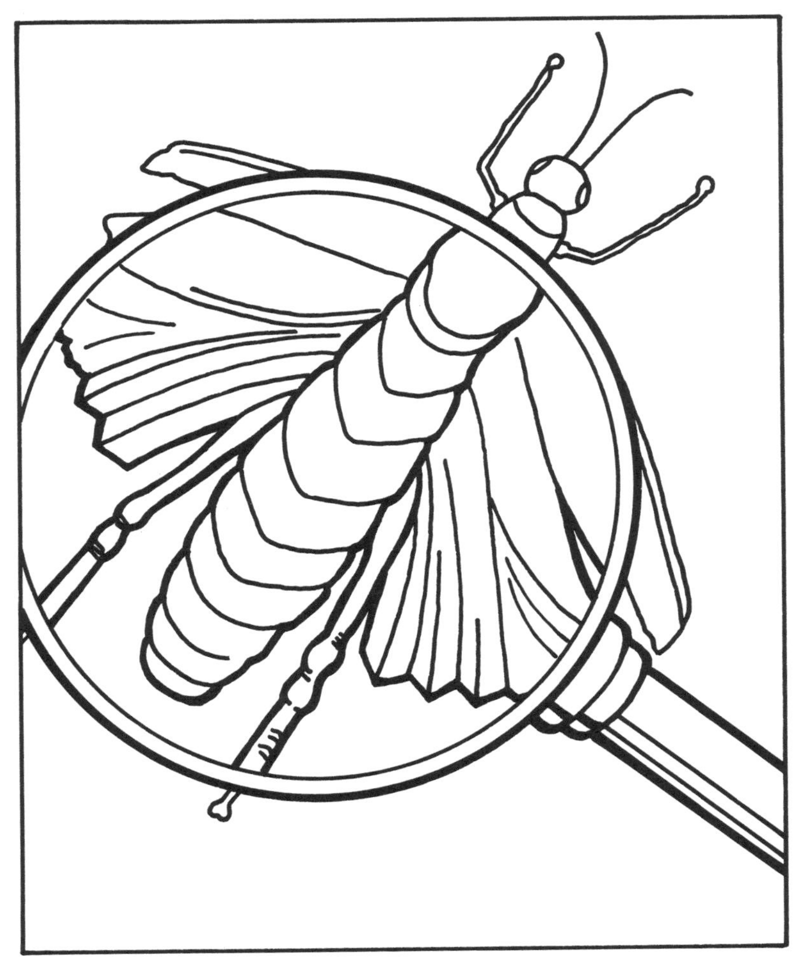

Crack Critters

In the concrete-covered areas of the city, animals sometimes find suitable habitats in even the smallest areas where soil might accumulate. Many displaced animals die in the city, but others manage to survive in a micro-world. This is an opportunity for students to observe the critters who have found a new niche in the city.

Relevance to Everyday Life

Micro-habitats exist in natural areas and may contain natural boundaries such as tree trunks and root bases. A crack in the sidewalk represents a similar type of micro-habitat. Have students list all the needs of the critters they find there. Allow them to speculate on how the critters fill those needs in a confined area such as a sidewalk crack. Ecology of limited resources is a principle which can be applied to humans as well, because we consume many resources faster than they can be replaced.

Materials

- ☐ Chalk
- ☐ Magnifying glasses (optional)
- ☐ Observation Books
- ☐ Pencils

How to Do It

Have each team adopt a sidewalk crack. It may be necessary to mark the crack in some way with the chalk. Be sure the marking is unobtrusive. Some students may need to be reminded that they are there to observe, not to disturb!

Data Collecting and Recording

Diagram the sidewalk crack, and make note of any life or signs of life which may be using it. This observation should be carried out numerous times a day over several days. Each team should keep a simplified journal of any activities observed along its sidewalk crack.

A team graph could be made showing the numbers of critter types found to be using the crack. What time of day is "rush hour" in the crack? A class graph based on each team's findings could be constructed. Is one area of sidewalk used more than another?

Extension Activities

- Ask students to compare the sidewalk cracks at the school to those near their homes or on the way to school.
- If a critter is seen, plot its path over and around the crack. Is it straight or does the critter backtrack and go in circles?
- Calculate the distance a critter travels, and the time it takes to go that distance. (Be sure to measure jags, circles, and backtracking!) What is the speed of the critter in miles per hour?

Name ______________________________

Crack Critters

Team ______________________________ Date ______________

Time ______________________________

Duplicate this page for each observation.

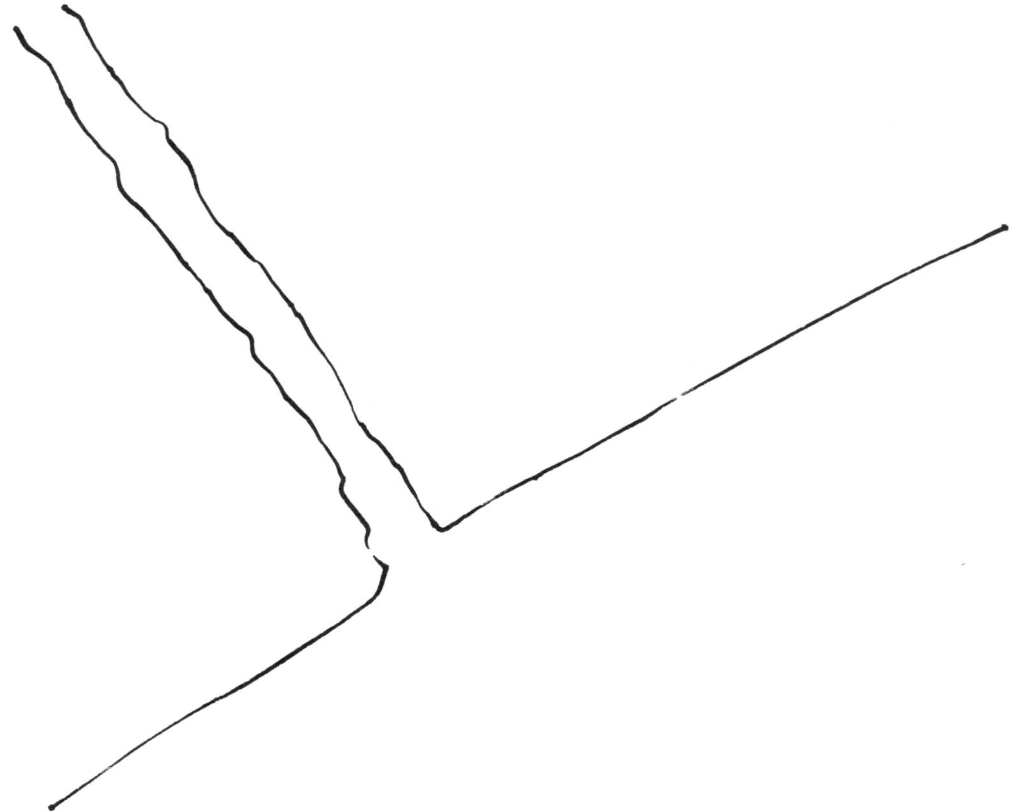

Draw everything you see. Try to draw objects to scale!

Name ______________________________

Crack Critters

Team ______________________________ Date ______________

Time ______________________________

How many of each critter did you find? You may want to compare your results with other teams. Duplicate this graph for each observation.

NUMBER OF CRITTERS

16								
15								
14								
13								
12								
11								
10								
9								
8								
7								
6								
5								
4								
3								
2								
1								
	Type A	**Type B**	**Type C**	**Type D**	**Type E**	**Type F**	**Type G**	**Type H**

TYPE OF CRITTER FOUND

Try to name the types of critters you found. Look in books on insects to help you with identification.

Type A = _____ Type D = _____

Type B = _____ Type E = _____

Type C = _____ Type F = _____

Did you find more? Identify them below.

Barking Up the Right Tree

Tree bark has distinct patterns, which can be used to help identify the tree. Diversity is a principle of nature that strengthens an ecosystem. Getting students to recognize tree types helps them understand that there are differences among objects that seem the same.

Relevance to Everyday Life

Diversity in ecosystems is essential to the health of the system. This activity helps students realize that there are recognizable differences in the bark of different trees. (Of course, the leaves are different as well, and if there are some available, you could make rubbings of them.) Bark also serves as the first line of defense for the tree, much like the protection our skin offers us. Discuss how removing bark harms the tree.

Materials

- ☐ Crayons with paper removed
- ☐ Ruler or craft stick
- ☐ Observation Books
- ☐ Pencils

How to Do It

Have each team choose a tree. Have each make a rubbing of the bark. With the ruler or craft stick, determine the depth of crevices, if any exist, in the bark.

Data Collecting and Recording

Each rubbing should be labeled with a code. Have teams exchange papers and measurements. Can they find the tree represented by the rubbing and measurement?

Extension Activities

- Ask students to make a tree-bark-rubbing notebook of other trees they might pass or have in their neighborhoods. This could be done over a span of several weeks.
- See if students can identify their teams' trees when blindfolded.
- Does each team's tree have a distinctive odor? Do all trees smell the same?

Name ______________________________

Barking Up the Right Tree

Team ______________________________ Date ______________

Code/Key* ______________________________

Tree Rubbing

Duplicate this page for each rubbing.

Be sure to use the SIDE of your crayon or pencil lead to make an accurate rubbing.

Depth of crevice in bark (use a craft stick or ruler to measure): _____

*If you make more than one rubbing, be sure to assign each rubbing a code number or letter. That way, you will be able to remember which rubbing comes from which tree.

Sound Advice

Animals communicate through sounds (calls) and movements. What sounds can your teams detect around the school grounds? Do the human-made sounds interfere with animal communication?

Relevance to Everyday Life

Ask students to imagine that they are animals (not the human type) living in the city. How could the human-made city sounds affect the quality of your life? Be very specific.

Materials

- ☐ Ears (attached to heads)
- ☐ Observation Books
- ☐ Pencils
- ☐ Tape Recorder with tape (optional)

How to Do It

Choose a "listening spot" for each team. Have teams sit or stand quietly for 10 to 15 minutes. Individual team members should record sounds on their own. Sounds should be placed in categories for ease of identification.

Data Collecting and Recording

Teams should create a chart or graph to represent the sounds they hear. If students are unfamiliar with specific bird calls, then "Bird 1," "Bird 2," "Bird 3" will suffice. Other categories may include "Engine Sound Type 1," "Engine Sound Type 2," "Female Voice 1," "Male Voice 2." Which sounds are more prevalent, nature's sounds or human-made sounds? What time of day is most noisy?

Extension Activities

- Compare the sounds and the frequency with which they occur from month to month throughout the year.
- Use a map of the city to pick out areas where sounds would be very different. If possible, visit those places.
- Reserve the gym, or other area in which noise can be contained. Play a record player or radio loudly (you may wish to choose songs or a style of music that is not liked by the students). Have students try to do different tasks; some that involve concentration, others that involve communicating, others that normally need quiet. Afterwards, discuss how the students felt. Would the results have been different if the activities had been done in the classroom? Why should "noise pollution" be controlled?

Sound Advice

Name ____________________

Time __________ Date __________

Listen carefully. What do you hear?

Sound Chart

Duplicate this chart for each time you collect sounds.

	TIMES HEARD	DIRECTION SOUND CAME FROM		
Bird I				
Bird II				
Bird III				
Engine I				
Engine II				
Voice I				
Voice II				
Wind				

Scent Sense

Most organisms have a highly developed sense of smell. Could the overabundance of human-made scents interfere with natural olfactory senses? Can students detect and identify the scents around their school?

Relevance to Everyday Life

Animals detect their young by smell, plants produce scents to attract pollinators (or to repel those who would eat them!) Which scents do you detect the most, natural or human-made? Do the human-made scents interfere with the scents of animals and plants?

Materials

- ☐ Observation Books
- ☐ Pencils
- ☐ Noses

How to Do It

Have teams go outside and sniff the air. Students should close their eyes to heighten the sense of smell. Teams should record any scents they receive by describing them. If they can identify the origin, it should be included.

Data Collecting and Recording

Keep a descriptive record of each scent, its source, and its intensity. A scale of 1 to 10 may be used with *1* being a very faint smell and *10* being a strong scent. Be sure to date each entry so that comparisons can be made throughout the year.

Extension Activities

- Carry out the study over the course of a month, or compare the scents counted from season to season, or morning to afternoon.
- Spray a strong, cheap perfume in the room. How do the students react? How long does it take for a small amount to permeate the room? How long does it take to "desensitize" their noses? This can be illustrated by leaving the room when the scent is no longer noticed, and then returning.
- Use old handkerchiefs to make scent bags. Make two of each scent. Some suggestions include cinnamon, garlic, cloves, peppercorns, and cotton dipped in vinegar. Five different scents is a good number with which to start. Choose one bag from each pair to form two identical sets. Thoroughly mix each set. Select five students to be animal babies. Give each "baby" one of the bags. Hold one bag from the other set near a student's nose. After smelling briefly, can they locate their "baby"—the one with the same scent? This activity can be made more difficult by using similar or more scents. Be sure that you can identify the two bags that belong together!

Name ______________________

Scent Sense

Team ______________________ Date ____________

Date	Scent Description	Intensity (1 - 10) *	Source (if known)	Wind Direction	Weather Conditions

*On a scale of 1-10, a scent that is very, very faint is a 1 and a scent that is very, very strong is a 10. Put a number from 1 to 10 in this column to indicate how intense the scent is.

Nature's Brushes

Seed pods have the job of ensuring the continuation of the species. Many pods are covered with bristlelike structures similar to the bristles on a paintbrush. Are there any of nature's brushes on your school grounds? Field teams will search for these brushes and observe the release mechanism each contains.

Relevance to Everyday Life

Seeds are the means by which Earth's life continues. They are designed to hold onto or conceal seeds until the perfect moment for release comes. Successful dispersal methods are essential for continued propagation of plant species. Ask students: Which plants will be the most successful? In the city, what are the chances that the seeds will find a fertile spot in which to grow?

Materials

- ☐ Assorted containers with lids
- ☐ Observation Books
- ☐ Pencils
- ☐ Seed pods

How to Do It

Have field teams find the seed pods of a variety of plants. Place only one of each type in a container. Seal the container and allow the pod to dry. If drying in this manner takes too long, dry the pods under a lightbulb, in a warm oven, or in a covered container in a microwave oven on LOW power.

Data Collecting and Recording

When the pods have opened, have each team count the number of seeds inside. Compare the number of seeds with other teams. Graph the number of seeds found in each type of pod. Glue one or two seeds from each variety onto the paper. Draw the seed pods.

Extension Activities

- Calculate how many seeds a particular plant releases in a season.
- Determine how many plants were examined and calculate the total number of seeds which could be released.
- Attempt to grow the released seeds. Determine the percent of those that develop.
- Make four identical seed-popping bags. Select one seed from each variety that was examined. Place seeds in self-locking plastic bags that each contain a moist paper towel. Tape one bag to each side of the building. Is one side of your school building more conducive for germinating seeds? Is one side of the building good for some seeds and bad for others?

Name ______________________________

Nature's Brushes

Team ______________________________ Date ______________

Pod Type	Sketch Closed Pod	Number of Seeds in Pod	Sketch Open Pod

*Use a scientific classification or just *Type I, II, III* for the Pod Type.

Name ______________________

Nature's Brushes

Team ______________________ Date ____________

NUMBER OF SEEDS								
32								
30								
28								
26								
24								
22								
20								
18								
16								
14								
12								
10								
8								
6								
4								
2								

TYPE OF SEED POD

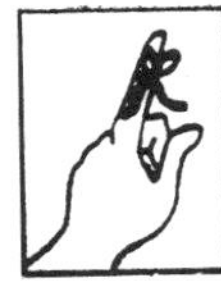

Don't forget to fill in the type of seed pods along the *x*-axis!

Flying Noses

Flying insects seem to be able to detect odors as soon as they are emitted (or so it seems). How fast can flying insects actually detect an odor after it is exposed to the open air? Students will find out as they attempt to lure flying insects to odors.

Relevance to Everyday Life

Flying insects are important as pollinators and distributors of variety among plants. However, anyone who has been on an outdoor picnic knows there are always uninvited guests in the form of certain flying insects. The speed with which these insects detect odors and find their source is phenomenal. Are there insects which are faster than others at detecting and finding the source of an odor? A tremendous number of insect repellents are available today to deter the invasions of these flying noses. Are the repellents really effective?

Materials

- [ ] One substance from the three categories below:
  Odor-producing foods (suggestions include peanut butter, marshmallows, apple pieces, orange sections)
  Odor-producing liquids (suggestions include lemonade, fruit punch, milk)
  Odor-producing materials (Some suggestions include hairspray, perfume, cleaning agents—use pump bottles, NOT aerosols)
- [ ] Small container with tight fitting lid
- [ ] Marker
- [ ] Stopwatch, or watch with second hand
- [ ] Observation Books
- [ ] Pencils

How to Do It

To make an "odor container," place a small amount of the odor-producing substance on the underside of the lid. Pour liquids directly into the container. Spray hairsprays or perfume directly into the cup, taking care NOT to get any on the outside of the container. Place the lid on the container tightly. This should seal the odor inside the container. Label each container so you know what is inside without opening the top.

Choose an outdoor site away from the lunch area (if you eat outside) and where student movement can be kept to a minimum. Have each team be responsible for a different odor. Predetermine the time you will leave the odor exposed. Start timing as soon as the lid is removed and placed underside up beside the container. With solid foods (such as peanut butter), turn the cup upside down before removing the lid so the odor is exposed. Shake liquids slightly to splash some onto the lid before opening.

 (continued on page 53)

𝍸 Data Collecting and Recording

After listing the source of the odor, expose the odor to the air and start the stopwatch. Observe the area for flying insects. Remember to stay back from the container. Record the time it takes for insects to appear. In addition to the time, be sure to note the type of flying insect. Keep a careful count if more than one of a particular insect appears.

If there is an abundance of flying insects in the area, you may have to vary the location for each odor. Be sure to seal all odor containers before moving! Try not to spill any contents! Compare the results with other teams. Did one type of insect appear more frequently? Which insect type was the quickest to appear?

✚ Extension Activities

- Carry out the study at various times during the year, such as early and late fall; early and late spring; a warm winter day. Compare number, type, and response time.
- Graph the response times of the insects. If possible, calculate the average response time for each kind of insect.
- Research the types of insects which are being attracted. Try to determine why they are equipped with such sensitive odor-detecting systems. How does this enable them to survive?
- After determining the most effective insect-attracting odors, attempt to make them less attractive by using a light coating of insect repellents. Use natural and artificial repellents if possible.

Name ____________________

Flying Noses

Team ____________________ Date ____________

Odor	Insect Type	Time to Respond	Number That Responded

Keep a sharp eye out as you try to discover what flying creatures are attracted to your odor!

Physical Science Activities

Let Me Down

Physics concepts can be difficult, even for college students. To help children feel more comfortable in the physical sciences, exposure is a must, starting in the elementary school. What better place to start than on the school playground?

Relevance to Everyday Life

For students of different weights to play together on a teeter-totter, the position of the fulcrum must be adjusted. Why?

Materials

- ☐ Teeter-totter
- ☐ Two identical boxes (such as a photocopier paper box) containing sand or dirt: one box half full, the other almost full
- ☐ Scale
- ☐ Tape measure
- ☐ Observation Books
- ☐ Pencils

How to Do It

Give each team two boxes with sand inside. Explain that the boxes are aliens that have come to investigate what school is like on earth. The aliens are particularly interested in a piece of playground equipment that looks like a board over a railing. They would like to "try it out." The team's job is to find a way for the aliens to do just that!

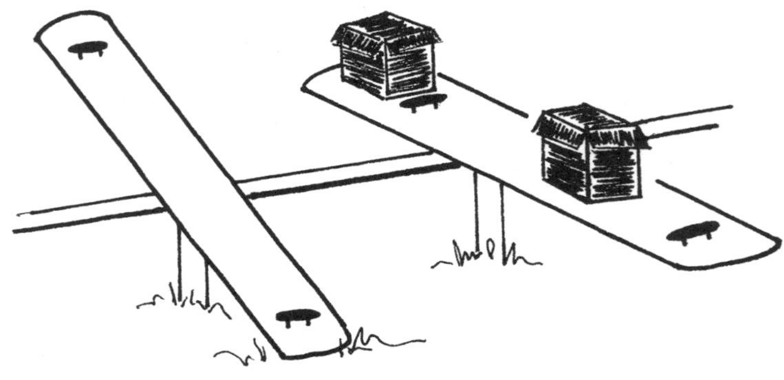

Data Collecting and Recording

Students should weigh and record the weight of both boxes. Measure the total length of the teeter-totter on your playground. A drawing can be made with this information recorded. Once the teeter-totter can balance with a box on each end, the investigative team should measure from the fulcrum (the point that it is attached to the support) to the closest end of each box.

For the aliens to be able to balance the teeter-totter, the force (in this case, weight) times the distance on one side of the fulcrum must equal the force (weight) times the distance on the other side. In physics, this is referred to as "summing the moments."

Extension Activities

- If the fulcrum is located in the center of the teeter-totter, where do the boxes need to be placed to balance?
- The teeter-totter is an example of a lever. In the room, have students make a lever using a board and a stack of books. Put some dictionaries in a box. Have students calculate where the fulcrum should be placed to lift the box. Then try it out!

Name ______________________________

Let Me Down

Team ______________________________ Date ______________

Fill in the weight of each box and the total length of the teeter-totter.

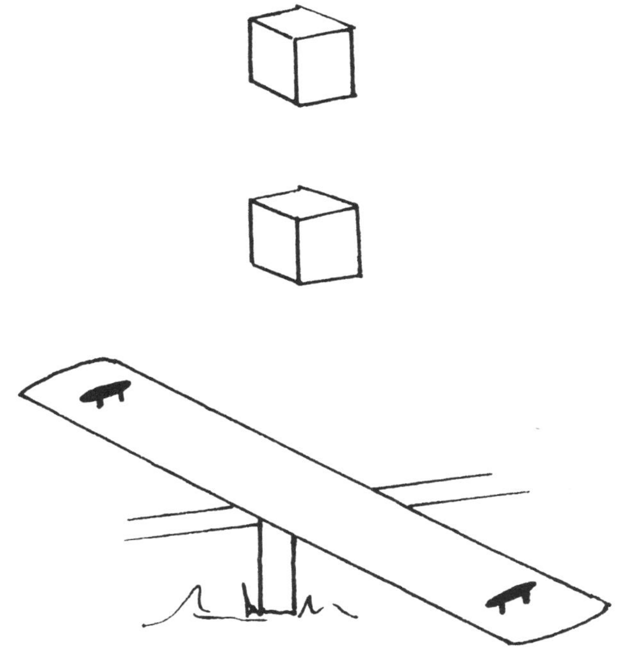

"How Things Looked"

Draw what the teeter-totter looked liked when the boxes were balanced. Be sure to include measurements!

Up, Up and Away

Where does rain come from? The answer to this question can be understood by studying the water cycle. In this activity, investigative teams will try to determine how the time of day affects evaporation rate.

Relevance to Everyday Life

During water rationing, restrictions are often placed on the time of day watering can take place. The rationale is that water evaporates at different rates during various times of the day. Why should you not water when the evaporation rate is high? Watering at what time of day allows the most water to reach the roots of the plants?

Materials

- ☐ 35 mm film container
- ☐ Plastic dish (such as a salad container from a fast food restaurant)
- ☐ Water
- ☐ Thermometer
- ☐ Stopwatch, or watch with second hand
- ☐ Observation Books
- ☐ Pencils

How to Do It

Fill the film container with water. Pour the water into the plastic dish. Set the dish at a designated location early in the school day. Repeat the activity at noon and again near the end of the school day.

Data Collecting and Recording

Each team needs to record the time of day, air temperature, other conditions such as the amount of sunlight, and how long it took for the water to evaporate. Evaporation rates will vary, depending on humidity and air temperature. Compare the results with other teams. What generalizations can be made from all the data gathered? During water rationing, when would the optimal time be to water? Why?

Extension Activities

- Repeat the activity at different times during the school year. How does temperature and humidity effect the results?
- What happens if water does not evaporate? Overwater a potted plant and observe the results.
- See the activity Dewdrops for another water cycle activity.

Name ______________________

Lab 1 Up, Up and Away

Team ______________________ Date ______________

Complete this chart for your class.

Team	Location	Time of Day	Temp.	Evaporation Time	Comments

What time of day does water evaporate fastest? Why?

Hot Colors

A trip into any clothing store will alert you to the season of the year. Not only are the kinds of fabrics distinct, colors are very different in the summer than they are in winter. Students will discover the science behind this color change as they participate in this investigation.

Relevance to Everyday Life

The color of the roof of a new building is not determined by the flip of a coin. In areas where sun is intense, what color should the roof be to reflect the most heat? Why? While traveling in the Arctic, what colors of clothing should you wear so that heat will be absorbed? Why?

Materials

- [ ] Thermometers with plastic or cardboard backing
- [ ] Fabric scraps (a variety of colors of the same fabric type)
- [ ] Observation Books
- [ ] Pencils

How to Do It

Set the thermometer in the sun. Cover the bulb of each thermometer with a fabric scrap. Thermometers should remain undisturbed for 5-10 minutes before the temperature is recorded.

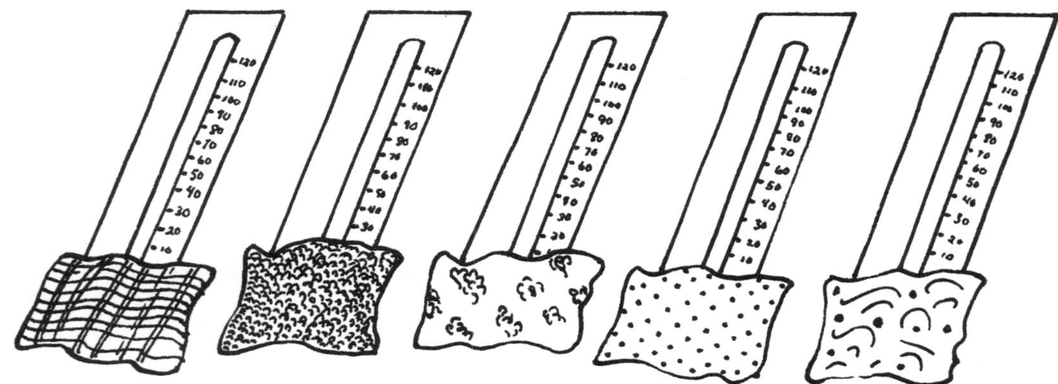

Data Collecting and Recording

For each thermometer, field teams should record the location, color of fabric and the temperature. Graphs could be made comparing the color of fabric to the temperature. How does color affect temperature? Which colors are more reflective (and therefore cooler)? Which colors absorb more light and heat?

Extension Activities

- Wrap a light color of a fabric around one arm, and a dark color of the same fabric around a different arm. Go out in the sunlight. What difference, if any, did you notice?
- Observe the ten buildings closest to your school. Which of the buildings will reflect the most heat from the sun? Why?
- Wear dark colors to school one day, light colors the next. How do you feel after recess? (Make sure that weather conditions are similar for the two days.)

Name ______________________________

Hot Colors

Team ______________________________ Date ______________

Location ______________________________

Now record this information on a bar graph.

TEMPERATURE

°								
°								
°								
°								
°								
°								
°								
°								
°								
°								
°								
°								
°								
°								
°								
	Control							

COLOR OF FABRIC

Fabric Color	Temperature
Control	

Fabric Color	Temperature
Control	

Don't forget to fill in the fabric colors and the degrees!

Swinging into Action

Use the playground to teach physics! A playground swing is the perfect place to introduce and reinforce the concept of frequency.

Relevance to Everyday Life

Frequency is an important part of our lives. Light waves travel in frequencies to our eyes. We hear sounds due to frequency of sound waves. Even our radios have *F.M.*, or *Frequency Modulated,* stations. On the radio dial, the higher the number, the higher the frequency. Look at the strings in a piano. Compare the length of the strings of higher pitched notes to the length of the strings of lower pitched notes?

Materials

- ☐ Playground swing
- ☐ Rope
- ☐ Protractor
- ☐ Tape measure
- ☐ Stopwatch, or watch with a second hand
- ☐ Observation Books
- ☐ Pencils

How to Do It

On the swing set, locate two swings of different lengths. Determine the angle the swings will start. Use a protractor to measure. Hold the swing, chains tight, at that angle. When the person timing says go, release the swing (do not push). Count the number of times the swing oscillates back and forth in one minute. A complete movement back and forth is counted as one. Repeat using the other swing.

Data Collecting and Recording

Measure the length of each swing. Record the angle at which the swings were released. Count and compare the frequencies of the swings in a one-minute period. Which swing had the lower frequency? Why?

Extension Activities

- Extend a plastic ruler four inches off the edge of a desk. Strike it and listen to the pitch. Increase the extended length to eight inches. Compare the pitch. How does length affect pitch? Do high pitches vibrate faster or slower than low pitches?
- Borrow a metronome from the music department. Have students predict the beat as the weight is moved up and down on the oscillating rod.

Name ______________________________

Swinging into Action

Team ______________________________ Date ______________

Angle of Swing ______________________

SWING NUMBER	LENGTH OF SWING	FREQUENCY

What relationship did you find between the length of the swing and its frequency?

Sliding into Science

Use the slide on your playground to introduce or reinforce what friction is and how it works. Your students will see how friction works firsthand, and get practice with measuring and comparing time.

Relevance to Everyday Life

In a car, too little friction in the brakes results in the car's inability to stop. On the other hand, too much friction in the engine will cause the engine to overheat. Brake shoes are rough, while engine oil makes engine parts slide smoothly past each other.

Materials

- [ ] Playground slide
- [ ] Shoe box
- [ ] Weighted object (suggestions include book, stapler, tape dispenser)
- [ ] Stapler with staples
- [ ] Materials to cover bottom of shoe box (Be sure to include waxed paper and sandpaper! Other suggestions: plastic bag, newspaper, dryer sheet, aluminum foil, satin fabric, corduroy fabric)
- [ ] Stopwatch, or watch with second hand
- [ ] Magnifying glass (optional)
- [ ] Observation Books
- [ ] Pencils

How to Do It

Wrap one of the "box coverings" around the bottom of the shoe box. Bring the edges of the covering over the sides and staple in place (four staples, two per side, are sufficient). Place the back edge of the box even with the beginning of the down slope of the slide. Place weight in the box.

Data Collecting and Recording

Release the shoe box (DO NOT PUSH). Time how long it takes the box to get to the bottom. Record the type of covering used on the box, and the time. Remove the covering and replace it with a different covering. Examine each covering. How would you describe it? Compare the recorded times with the coverings. What correlations can be made? (Some coverings may prevent the box from sliding down the slide. This should be noted as well.)

Extension Activities

- Ask a service station for a variety of old car brakes. Examine the brakes. What do the brakes have in common? What are the differences? If possible, secure a new pair of brakes and compare them to the used brakes.
- Repeat the activity with different sizes of boxes and/or different weights in the box. Are the results the same?

Name ______________________

Sliding into Science

Team ______________________ Date ____________

Covering on Box	Time to Go Down

Now make a bar graph of your findings. Be sure that all your labels are in the right place!

TIME

COVERING ON BOX

Rolling Along

Looking for a different activity to get your students rolling in a unit on machines? Use a five- or ten-speed bicycle to show how gears work.

Relevance to Everyday Life

Many of the bicycles sold today have more than one gear. The lower gears make hill climbing easier, while higher gears can make it easier to ride on flat stretches. The ratio of the pedal to the gear is what makes the difference.

Materials

- ☐ Five- or ten-speed bicycle
- ☐ Fluorescent tape
- ☐ Observation Books
- ☐ Pencils

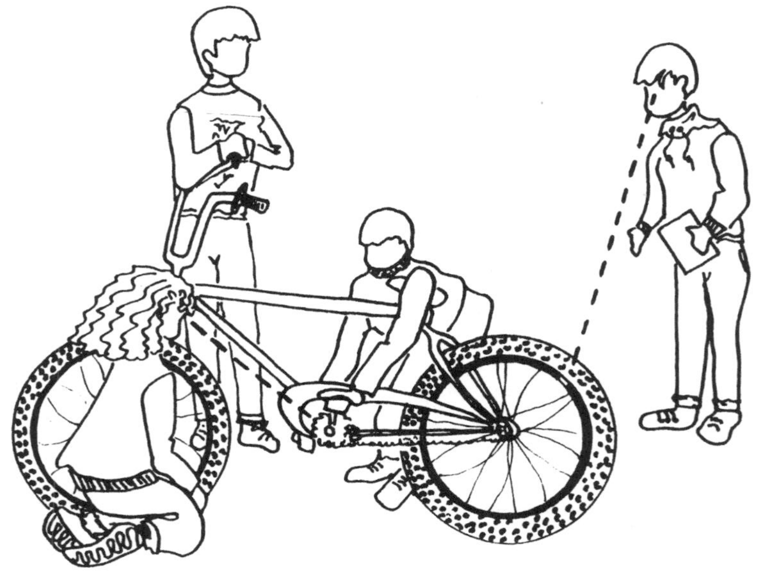

How to Do It

In this investigation, teams will be comparing the revolutions of a bicycle's pedals to the revolution of its back tire. To make counting the revolutions easier, attach a piece of fluorescent tape to the rim of the back wheel. One team member is responsible for notifying the team when the back tire has made one complete revolution. Another team member is responsible for moving the pedals of the bike. A third team member is responsible for counting the number of revolutions the pedals make. A fourth member helps to steady the bike, if necessary.

Start with the bicycle in the lowest gear. Walk the bicycle, moving the pedals by hand at the same time. Count the number of times the pedal must go around to move the back tire one revolution.

Data Collecting and Recording

When the back tire has made a complete revolution, stop and record the gear and the number of revolutions made by the pedals (you may need to discuss fractional parts of a circle). Repeat the activity with each gear on the bicycle. Compare the results. How does the gear affect the number of pedal revolutions per back-tire revolution?

Extension Activity

- Compare different bicycles. Is the relationship between the revolution of the back tire and the pedals the same?

Name ______________________

Lab 1 Rolling Along

Team ______________________ Date ______________

Type of bicycle ______________________

For each gear on the bicycle, how many times must the pedal revolve (go around) for the back wheel to go around once? Record your results on this chart.

GEAR NUMBER	PEDAL ROTATIONS
1	
2	
3	
4	
5	
6	
7	
8	
9	
10	

Recommended gear for riding on a flat terrain: _____

Recommended gear for riding up a hill: _____

Survey Science

Cloudy Cover

We are "covered" by clouds daily, but rarely look close enough to infer relationships between clouds and the prevailing weather patterns. This survey will allow students to observe cloud types over a period of time and then to compare the types to actual weather patterns. Who knows—they may even predict the weather!

Relevance to Everyday Life

Clouds are moving masses of condensing water vapor, which usually bring with them a change in weather conditions. They line up along the leading edge of a new weather front and enclose us when the full system surrounds our location. Meteorologists use clouds as they appear from satellite photos to identify weather systems. Because they have had repeated exposure, sailors and outdoor people understand the messages clouds send. Regular observations will help your students to see the relationships between clouds and weather patterns.

Materials

- ☐ Cloud charts (usually available through education catalogs)
- ☐ Observation Books
- ☐ Pencils

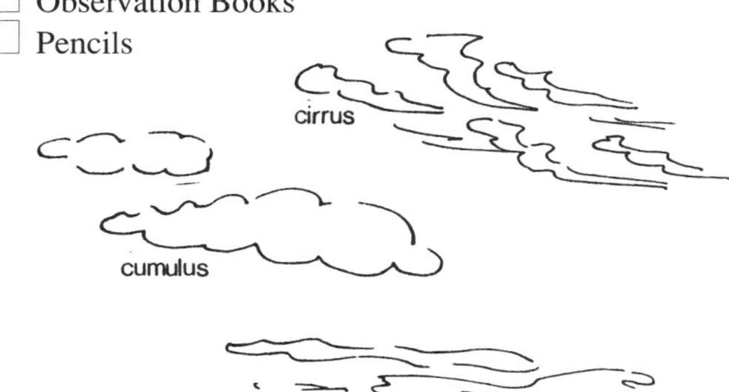

How to Do It

Observe the clouds from a location that allows a full view of the sky. Teams should always use the same location when making observations. Plan this activity when you know weather systems are moving into your area. This will provide the motivation to keep it an ongoing survey.

Data Collecting and Recording

Students should sketch clouds as they appear from the team's location. Cloud types should be labeled. Teams may try to calculate the percent of cloud cover by comparing clouds to blue or non-cloudy areas. Field teams should keep records for at least five consecutive days or throughout the movement of the system. A more meaningful relationship can be inferred between cloud cover and weather patterns if several surveys are made. Ideally, a week each month should be dedicated to collecting cloud cover data. Display the week's observation pages so that the overall cloud picture can be seen.

Extension Activities

- Correlate outside temperature to the cloud cover. Draw inferences from these observations. Is there a relationship?
- Test the old adage "the fifth rules the month." Record weather statistics on the fifth of the month. How do they compare to the statistics for the rest of the month?
- Research and report on the greenhouse effect, comparing it to cloud cover.
- Write to NOAA for prints of their satellite cloud photographs. How do they compare to observations made from the schoolyard?
- Invite a meteorologist to your classroom. How is the weather reported to the public? What training is necessary to become a meteorologist?
- Prepare a schoolwide weather report. Broadcast the next day's weather over the school's public address system.

Name ______________________________

Lab 1 Cloudy Cover

Team ______________________________ Date ______________

The square below represents the entire sky as you can see it. Sketch the clouds you see. Shade in the cloud shapes lightly. Duplicate this chart for each day clouds are observed.

North

West **East**

South

Place this chart over a piece of quadrille paper. Count the number of squares covered by a shaded area. How many squares are covered?____

As a challenge, can you determine the percentage of cloud cover? (Hint: compare the number of squares covered by a shaded area to the squares that are not covered by a shaded area. Use only the squares inside the chart's border.)

Yellow Pages Science

In your community, who are the scientists or the people who use science in their daily jobs? Students will survey the yellow pages directory in an attempt to locate and categorize the science-related professions and businesses.

Relevance to Everyday Life

Science surrounds us in our daily lives, but students often miss the connection. The obvious professions include physicians, dentists, pharmacists, and engineers. But what about the hidden application of science in computers, electricity, mechanics, heating, plumbing, radio, TV, telephone, welding, and so on? Can your students find the businesses and associated professions that utilize the principles of science (applied science)?

Materials

- ☐ Yellow pages (Have one book for each team. Perhaps you could ask the students to bring the books from home or write to the telephone company for additional copies.)
- ☐ Observation Books
- ☐ Pencils

How to Do It

Each team should go through the yellow pages directory and make a list of all the businesses that rely on scientific principles.

Data Collecting and Recording

After the lists (which may be quite long) are made, have teams categorize the scientific application (medicine, engineering, physics, chemistry, and so on) and count the numbers. Depending on your class, you may need to give one example for each category to get students started. From this information, the teams can determine the type of science that is most prevalent in the community.

Extension Activities

- Send for the yellow pages from other cities and compare the types of science-related businesses. Does the size or location of the city have any affect on the results?
- Relate each business to a profession or job type that calls for training in a science or applied-science area.
- Survey parents within the class to determine what percentage hold occupations that rely on scientific principles.
- Invite a representative of each business type to your class for a "Science Careers Day." Ask them to talk about preparation necessary to do their jobs or run their businesses.

Yellow Pages Science

Team ____________________

Date ____________

Put all the science-related businesses you found in the yellow pages in the appropriate category. Some may fit into more than one category.

Medicine	Engineering	Earth	Physics	Chemistry	Computer Science	Botany	Zoology	Environmental Science

Bright Lights

Our city life goes on after dark due in part to the lighting that lines our streets and glows on building fronts. The type of light used is usually based on the purpose of the light. Students will take a survey of the types of lighting used by the city and the physical characteristics of each type.

Relevance to Everyday Life

Since the invention of fire, humans have been able to go forth into the darkness of night. Electric, gas, and vapor lights now replace the torchlights of the past. Some city locations appear to be "as bright as day." The invention of the light bulb and recent methods of producing light have changed our nighttime lifestyles. What types of lights are found in your city? How do they affect the people around them?

Materials

- [ ] A map of the area surrounding your school
- [ ] A map of the city (optional)
- [ ] Tape measure
- [ ] Observation Books
- [ ] Pencils

How to Do It

Assign each team to a street leading to your school. The teams are responsible for counting, drawing, and measuring the distance from light to light for their particular streets.

Data Collecting and Recording

Each team should draw a map to scale of their street or assigned area. Careful measurements should be made (if measuring devices are not available, use "pacing" after a standard pace has been determined). Each streetlight should be drawn, and the distance from one light to the next indicated. A careful diagram should be made clearly shows the appearance of the streetlight. You may need to use a small pair of binoculars to see detail on the light. If possible, determine the height of the light by using the "artist's method" (see the Appendix for directions). Graph and compare the results of the streetlight survey.

Extension Activities

- Have team members survey their own neighborhood streetlights in the same way. Be sure the measurements are made in the same manner. Use the city map to locate the areas surveyed. Add these streets to the class graph.
- Write to the power company in your city asking for information on light placement, light height, and types of lights used. Include a diagram of the type of lights you have surveyed and ask for a technical picture of the same lights. Ask if a representative is available to visit your school and share more information with your class.
- Use the city map and the results from your survey to determine how many streetlights there are in your city. Of course, you'll need to determine how many miles of streets there are and calculate the number of lights per mile. Have a contest between the teams, then write to the power company for the answer!
- Calculate the cost of operating the lights by first determining the rate per kilowatt-hour. This rate is usually listed on an electric bill (if not, then call your local electric company). Then find out the number of kilowatts generated by the streetlights. Use the relationship *cost = rate* x *wattage*.

Name ______________________

Lab 1 Bright Lights

Team ______________________ Date __________

Street or area ______________________

Draw the lights along the street. Use a scale to indicate distances. For example, 1 inch on your drawing may equal 10 feet along the street. This scale is shown as 1 in. = 10 ft, or 1:120.

Scale used _____

Name ______________________

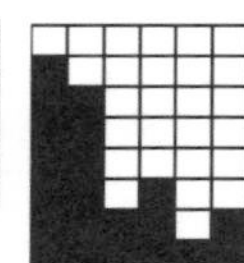

Bright Lights

Date ____________

Do all the streets around your school have the same number of lights? Compare your team's findings with those of others. Which street has the most lights? Why?

NUMBER OF LIGHTS

16								
15								
14								
13								
12								
11								
10								
9								
8								
7								
6								
5								
4								
3								
2								
1								

STREETS

Don't forget to fill in the names of the streets that were surveyed!

Window Watchers

Windows of all types are usually evident as we look around at the cityscape and the buildings that surround us. Some appear small, and some seem to cover the entire building. Your teams will survey the types and sizes of windows that they see in the city and attempt to assess their value.

Relevance to Everyday Life

Offices and rooms "with a window" seem to be at a premium. Everyone wants to be able to see outside, and to have some natural light to brighten their day. While the appearance of the building may be the primary consideration for window placement, research has proven that natural light improves our well-being, and that we should each be bathed in bright, natural light for at least part of each day.

Materials

- ☐ Observation Book
- ☐ Pencils
- ☐ Tape measure

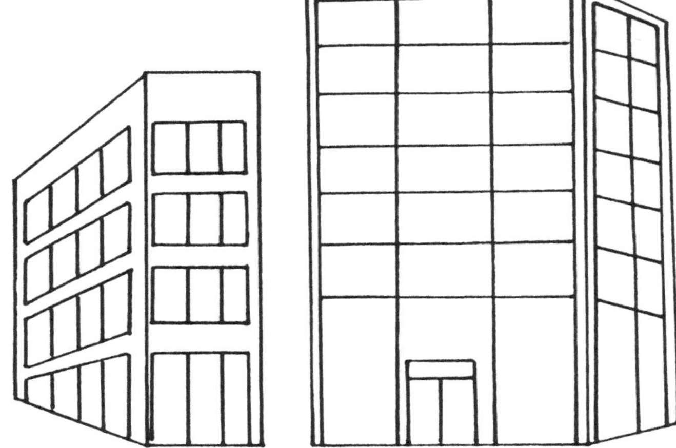

How to Do It

Assign a building or specific part of a building to each team of students. You may want to start with the school itself (if it has windows). Have students count the windows from the outside and measure those that appear to have a standard size. They may do an inside survey to see which rooms have windows and which do not.

If surveying buildings at a distance from the school, count the windows that can be seen and estimate the total number.

Data Collecting and Recording

Sketch each building and the windows that have been counted. Construct a chart to compare the numbers of windows in the buildings. Hang each sketch in a position within the classroom to create a "cityscape" as it is seen from the school.

Extension Activities

- Determine the amount of actual window area in relation to the building itself (*Area = base x height*). For distant buildings, write to the appropriate building maintenance department for window size and building height.
- Initiate a study of window tinting. Determine whether any of the windows on the buildings you have surveyed use tinted windows. Use a light meter to compare the amount of light passing through an untinted window to the same window with a piece of tinting attached (use tape for a temporary installation).
- Write to a few of the businesses that are housed in the buildings. Survey their feelings concerning windows. Do they like them or not? How many of the occupants have an office with a window?
- Carry out a survey of the families of students in your grade level or within the entire school. Find out how many of the adults have windows in their immediate work areas. How do they feel about the windows?

Name ______________________

Lab 1 Window Watchers

Team ______________________ Date ____________

Cityscape

Sketch your building below. Be sure to include all of the windows that have been counted or measured. Include in your sketch the buildings that are on each side of your building.

Name ______________________

Lab 2 Window Watchers

Team ______________________ Date ______________

Window Watchers Chart

*If your building has a name, write it in this column. If it does not, give your building a number or name. Be sure to identify it on your Cityscape Drawing.

Building *	Number of Windows	Window Shape (draw or describe)	Size of Window

Don't forget to include the unit of measure (inches or centimeters, for example) with the window size!

Who's Winging It

Our fine feathered friends travel each fall and spring to areas of the country for wintering and nesting. City dwellers sometimes miss the wing beats and songs, which can become lost in the cacophony of city sounds. Unless a concerted effort is made to sight these winged ones, their presence may go unnoticed. Students will attempt to survey populations of bird life within the city (yes, even pigeons).

Relevance to Everyday Life

As any "birder" will tell you, birds are an indication of the health of the environment in a particular area. If birds can't or don't choose to live there, it is time to question the quality of the environment in that location. Loss of habitat (favorable living area) is another reason birds may vacate an area. It may even forecast the demise of a species and its eventual extinction. What kinds of birds are evident in your city? Are they the same as in the past, or has the type of bird life changed over the years? Could this indicate a change in the environmental conditions of the area?

Materials

- [ ] Bird book, or pictures of birds
- [ ] Record or tape of birdcalls or bird songs (optional)
- [ ] Observation Books
- [ ] Pencils

How to Do It

Introduce this survey at a time of year when the most birds will be present (usually late summer or early spring). Give the teams an idea of the types of birds that may be seen in the area surrounding the school. The library should be able to supply you with bird books and may even have a tape of calls or songs.

Survey the types and numbers of birds that are seen in specific areas around the school and along the routes children take home. If the overhead wires provide a roosting area for birds, make careful counts and plan to survey these locations weekly over several months. Be sure that each team keeps careful records. Have each team prepare sketches of the types seen.

(continued on page 81)

𝍸 Data Collecting and Recording

Each team should create and keep a chart of the birds seen over the course of the survey time (day, week, month). Pictures correspond to the birds being identified should be posted around the room, or small pictures of each type could be duplicated and used to graph the actual numbers seen. Team data should be transferred to a class graph depicting the types and numbers counted.

✚ Extension Activities

- Research each type of bird seen and attempt to follow its life cycle. Determine its food source, its habits, and its behavior patterns (is it a migrating bird?).
- Interview people who have lived in the city for many years. Try to determine how the bird populations have changed over the years. Show the interviewees pictures of birds to identify types that may no longer be present.
- Prepare a class bird booklet, "City Birds in the Fall" (or spring), composed of survey sheets, pictures, and information gathered by the students. Include a section on birds of the past (if you have interviewed longtime residents). Some students may want to try to form a hypothesis explaining what has driven the birds away, or how to bring them back.

Name ______________________________

Who's Winging It

Date ______________

Date	Bird Type *	Number	Location Sited **

*If a bird cannot be identified, call it Type I, Type II, and so on, and then describe it.

**Where was the bird seen? On a tree? Wire? Pole? In flight?

Name ______________________

Who's Winging It

Date ______________

This graph can be done by the day, week, or month. Go bird-watching more than one time and compare sightings.

NUMBER OF BIRDS

16								
15								
14								
13								
12								
11								
10								
9								
8								
7								
6								
5								
4								
3								
2								
1								

TYPE OF BIRD

Use names, pictures, or drawings for the type of birds.

Appendix

Using Quadrille Paper

When using quadrille paper, simply place the drawing, circle, or irregular shape over the quadrille paper, hold it up to the light, and count the squares covered by the diagram. An alternate technique (especially useful for younger or beginning students) is to place the quadrille paper over the drawing, circle, or shape, and shade the squares that are covered by the figure. Count the shaded squares. Use quadrille paper to determine the percent of cloud cover in Cloudy Cover, and in Dewdrops to determine that amount of dew collected.

Graphs

A graph is used to illustrate relationships. The data collected will always be represented on the graph either as a bar indicating numbers or as a line indicating change. A bar graph will show the difference noted by each team. A line graph will show how those differences changed. The Observation Book pages provided indicate which type of graph is being called for.

Interviews

Before sending students out to conduct interviews with residents (Who's Winging It?) or with parents and businesses (Bright Lights), discuss the types of questions which need to be included. These should be written out as a guide for the students to use during the interview.

Artist's Method of Determining Height

To determine the height of the streetlights in Bright Lights, your students can use this simple method. Have a student of known height stand by the streetlight to be measured. This student is the "unit of measure."

Hold a stick or pencil at arm's length. Sight over the top of the stick to the head of the "unit of measure." Place your thumbnail on the stick where the line of sight meets the student's foot.

Determine the number of times the "unit of measure" fits into the streetlight by moving the stick upwards a unit at a time. Multiply that number by the height of the "unit of measure." This will give you the height of the streetlight.

This technique can be used whenever a tall object needs to be measured.

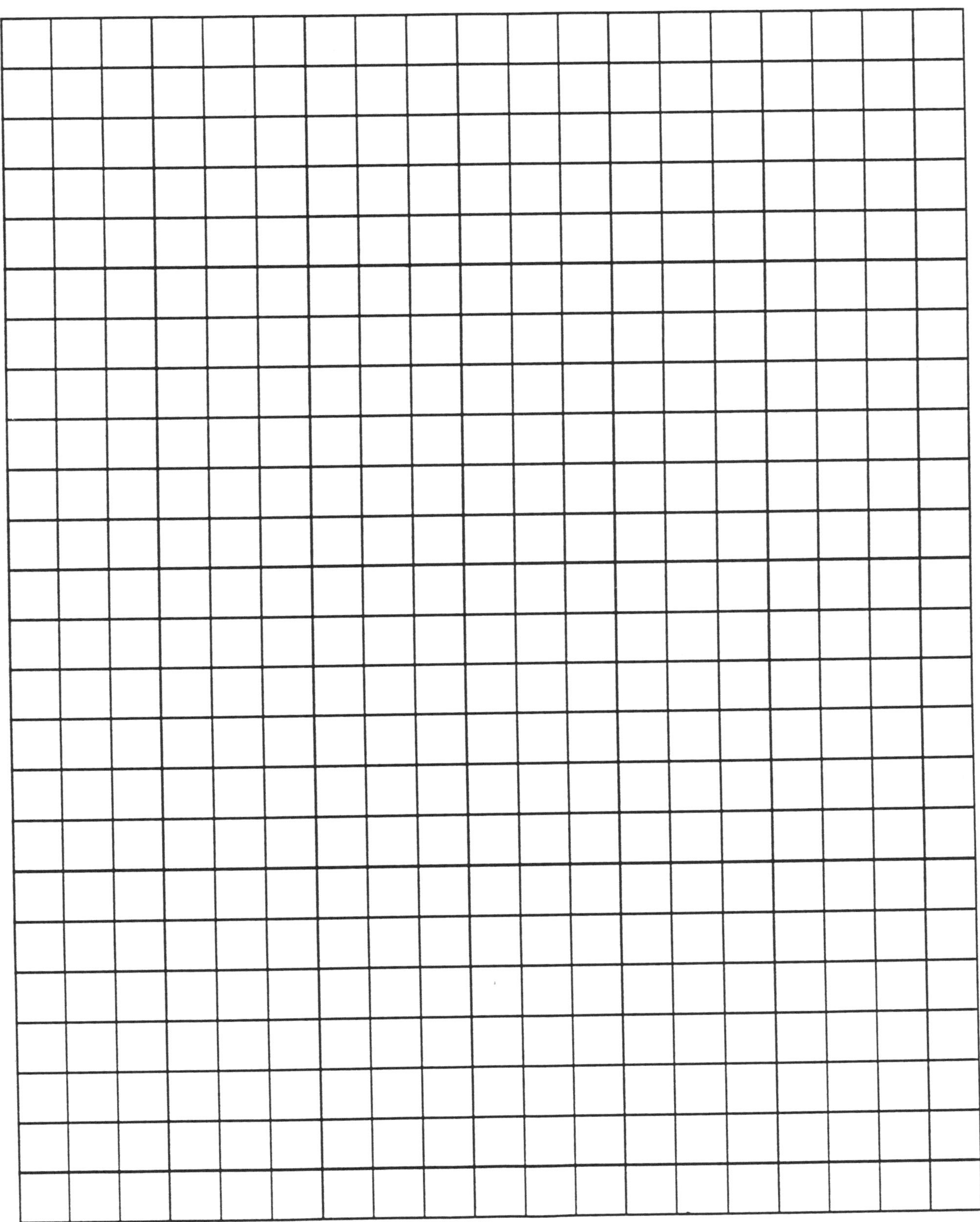

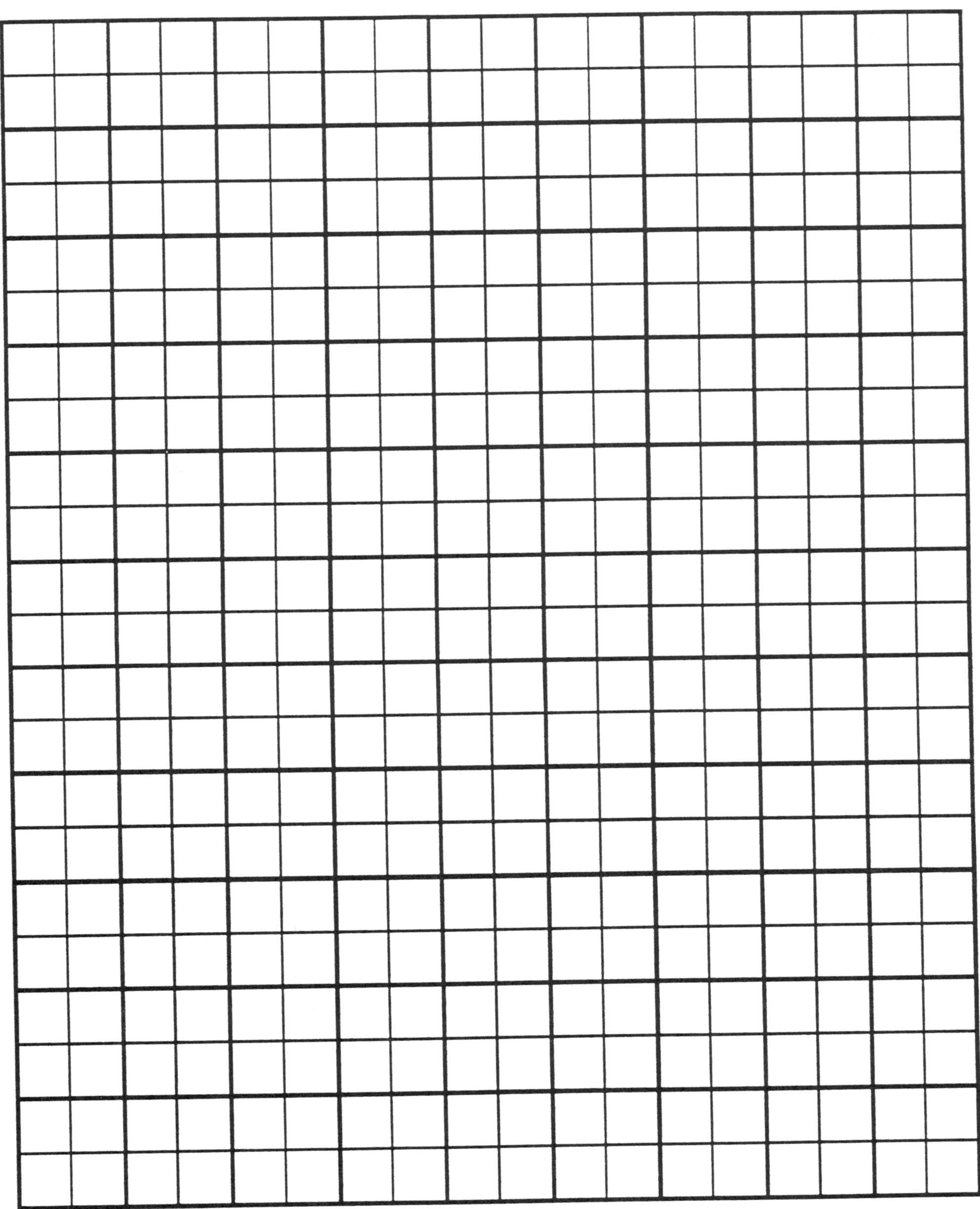

Observation Book
Table of Contents

Title	Page